Over 1000
CONTEMPORARY
POLITICAL POSTERS

by
Gary Yanker

Darien House, Inc. New York City

Distributed by New York Graphic Society, Ltd., Greenwich, Connecticut 06830

For Omi

Design: Harry Chester

Standard Book Number 8212-0426-2
Library of Congress Catalogue Card Number 79-189242
Printed in the United States of America

PROP ART

TABLE OF CONTENTS

PART II — THE POSTER GALLERY

Author's Notes
and Acknowledgements

It has been five years since I first began collecting posters. The idea for a book, however, did not occur to me until two years later. Therefore some of the documentation is uneven and incomplete. I tried later to identify these posters, but sometimes unsuccessfully; political posters are the most difficult posters to document. Political artists often do not sign or date their works. After the event which inspires the poster, the group sponsoring it is frequently disbanded. Also, many posters are a product of team work and a designer may well feel that the idea is more important then his own identity. Often the posters will be illegally posted, and so sponsors choose anonymity to avoid being implicated.

For the sake of some semblance of order in this collection, posters have been arranged in descriptive categories, some of which may seem a bit arbitrary. There are no neat compartments for convictions, therefore no rigid classifications for the poster interpreting these convictions. One man's peace poster is another man's anti-establishment poster.

Although incomplete, this collection can still serve as an inspiration for both the artist and the collector. For the artist, I humbly suggest that the posters shown here might become the source of new art styles. As Pop Art had its stylistic roots in commercial advertising, so a new art movement, possibly titled Prop Art, might draw its inspiration from political propaganda. The means and even the validity of such a movement or style, I leave entirely to the artist.

In any case, the political artist may use this book as a source of ideas for designing posters for small groups that cannot afford to hire an advertising firm to create their posters. The poster is the best form of communication for these groups because it is inexpensive and easily accessible. The artist, therefore, should use the guidelines and illustrations in this book to assure that the organization gets the best poster design possible.

Collectors might also be inspired by the vast amount of posters shown here. Political groups are often caught up in the passion of events and unable to save their own posters. If the collector does not intervene, many posters will be lost forever. The reader is therefore urged to become the curator of today's political posters.

I hope to regularly update my collection and to publish supplemental volumes as the supply of new posters dictates. I therefore invite interested readers and collectors to exchange ideas and posters with me.

I am indebted to my editor, Nancy Park, for the tremendous effort and keen personal interest which she brought to this project.

I also wish to give special thanks to the following individuals who helped me create this book: Harry Chester, Herbert Collins, Marty Fox, John Garrigan, Dr. Howard Penniman, Nicky Powell, Janet Rosen and Jack White.

My thanks also to Bill Aller, Richard Anobile, Valerie Beale, Richard Beyer, Laura Bigman, Joan Carrol, Dr. Karl Cerny, Gennaro Fernandez, Al Fusco, Peter Hanratty, Bob Hauser, Gertrude Von Hilgendorff, Kathryn Jellinek, Jerry Kretschner, John d'Arc Lorenz, Michael Manley, Robert Morton, Maleen Pacha, Helen Peterson, Jim Powell, Vivian Rowan, Alex Soma, Maria Teresa Ugarte, David Wenman, Elizabeth Yanker, Kristin Yanker.

— Gary Yanker
New York City
March, 1972

Introduction

It is a pleasure to be associated with this book, for a number of reasons. One of them is that it is, in the main, as contemporary as the stories I was covering only recently. Another reason is that I am a poster collector, although not as political, passionate, courageous, determined or scholarly as Gary Yanker. I have stuck up posters on the walls of motels, hotels, offices, on the back of my car (a get-out-the-vote bumper-sticker in Vietnamese) and for many years, in several homes, our living room has been dominated by a Max Bill poster for an exhibition of the works of Marcel Duchamp.

Long ago I decided that I could never afford originals of great art; and not being willing to settle for reproductions, I turned to maps, drawings, charts and posters — original, authentic art, and, to someone who spent much of his life travelling professionally from event to event, memorable art in the original sense of the word.

And now I discover the world of the collector of political posters. I have seen many political posters in my time, from Hong Kong to Moscow to Montreal, but I collected only a few, and those I bought. I thought it was either against the law to tear them down, or dangerous to get them from demonstrators. I find in Gary Yanker's text the rules of the game of collecting political posters, and the game is, often, either against the law or dangerous, even foolhardy. When I was a young police reporter you often had to steal pictures of the dead and injured from their families (and return them later); Gary Yanker's collector friends take bigger risks than that.

In this book, you will find Czech posters smuggled across borders; posters printed in the night by rebellious students in Paris; a poster purloined from militant Black Panthers — and Gary Yanker's story of the poster of Nasser he couldn't get because of a potentially murderous crowd in Cairo. So, it is not easy to put together a collection of a thousand recent political posters, and even though Gary Yanker says modestly it is only a handful of the posters produced since 1967, it is the only collection of its kind in the world.

It is a further pleasure for me to be associated with this book because I spent 40 days in Paris during the upheavals of May and June, 1968, when many of the best political posters of our time were being produced. I visited, often, during those days, the studios in the Ecole des Beaux-Arts where these famous designs were being turned out at night, to be torn down by the police the next day. These posters, some elegant, many crude, all effective, will always remind me more of France during *Les Journées de Mai* than any Cognac, any smell of a Gauloise. I wish I had been smart enough to steal a few more of those. They are hard to come by today, although a few of the smaller ones vibrated on our kitchen bulletin board for almost a year.

During these years of the late 1960's, we had the Six-day war in the Middle East; the collapse of France; the Viet Nam elections; the separatist French movement in Canada; the growth of anti-war opposition in the United States. I covered most of these stories, and saw the posters on the wall, some produced by governments, some (and usually the best) produced by rebels. Many of the best are in this book. (Some day someone ought to write, and illustrate, a book about slogans *painted* on walls, with brush or spray can. Like the one seen painted at the entrance to airports in Latin America, reading, in the local language, "Will the last one to leave the country please turn out the lights?" But political *graffiti* is another subject: we are dealing here with something which falls between art and politics, and ought to blend the best of both.)

There is a case to be made that the "poster phenomenon" has come about because motion pictures and, especially, television have heightened man's pictorial experience. After all, don't television-watchers these days produce posters? Don't young people in many countries have Che or Mao or a Black Panther on their wall? Aren't bookstores in most cities cashing in on the poster market? Hasn't Peter Max made a million on his mindless *kitsch*? Isn't this because we all have been brainwashed by visual images?

But there is also a case to be made that the success of posters has been possible not *because* of films and TV, but in opposition to, or rebellion against, films and TV. The big media images belong to everybody: Chairman Mao on the wall is *my* statement. It belongs to me.

Eugene McCarthy is an American politician who had, at one time, a unique ability to excite young people. Yet, we never see McCarthy posters on walls in American rooms or offices. How many Willy Brandts? Cohn-Bendits? Perhaps Che and Mao are on the walls because they have been quite outside the mainstream in North America and Europe and in the universities of the Middle East and Africa. Their images seem genuinely rebellious, so their faces are up in all sorts of places, as demonstrations of the (safe) rebelliousness of the people who stick up those posters.

Hang a poster and you say something about yourself. Something audacious. Which is why Richard Nixon, Edward Heath and Georges Pompidou are never going to be poster images, except in satire. Cesar Chavez, a saintly American rebel, yes; De Gaulle, no.

I believe this trend toward personal expression is just beginning, because the mass media are still dominant. People need outlets for individual expression, and especially people who think, or know, a bit more than the average about the world in which they live.

With this book, you have the first of its kind, but surely not the last. Read carefully what Gary Yanker writes about the Cyr, Picard people in Washington, who seem to have amassed a wicked lot of knowledge about posters; look carefully at the Chinese posters, for Peking knows what it means to be yellow, red, brown or black; think carefully about the old historical posters Gary Yanker has collected, since basic principles are basic principles; and rejoice that the fusion of art, polemics, color, painting, passion and commitment can result in so many expressions, for bad and good, of man's desire to get something up on a wall. Roofs are for shelter. Walls are for expression. If the pen is greater than the sword, the wall may be greater than the wheel.

John Chancellor
January, 1972
Washington, D.C.

GARY YANKER, born in New York City, spent four and one-half years studying and traveling throughout Europe and North Africa, receiving a diploma from the East European Institute in Switzerland and a degree in political science from Georgetown University in Washington, D.C. His interest in political posters stems from a poster display he saw as a student in Leningrad in 1967; and since that time, aided by his fluency in German, French and Russian, he has collected posters on a world-wide basis. In 1968 he founded the World Political Parties Institute for the purpose of enlarging and systematizing his collecting activities, and he now maintains contacts all over the world, corresponding regularly with more than 500 political parties and 3,000 pressure groups. Mr. Yanker has written articles on posters for *Print* and *World Affairs* magazines. He lives in New York, and is working toward degrees in law and business administration at Columbia University.

JOHN CHANCELLOR is anchorman for the daily NBC Television Network "Nightly News." Formerly National Affairs correspondent for NBC News, Mr. Chancellor has a wide range of experience in reporting national and international developments. In addition to domestic assignments, from space shots to presidential elections, he has also served extensively overseas in NBC News bureaus in Vienna, London, Moscow, Brussels and Berlin. From 1965 until 1967, as a Presidential appointee, he was Director of the Voice of America.

Foreword

About this Collection

Most of the posters in this book were taken from my personal collection, which includes over 3,000 pieces from 47 countries and represents five years of collecting. Although, to my knowledge, this is one of the world's largest collections of contemporary posters, compared to collections of the World War I and World War II period, it is relatively small. Some of these older collections contained as many as 28,000 pieces. The present collection is unique, however, in that it only contains political posters; it is not limited to a few countries, and, most importantly, it is recent. Political events move so quickly today that very few people are willing to take the time to record them in detail by preserving their documents. Existing institutions have been unable to mount a political poster collection effort similar to mine because they lack a comprehensive, economical, and centralized system of receiving posters as they are issued. If not collected immediately, political posters will disappear. Museums usually are not active collectors; they rely on donations by private collectors. German war posters, for example, entered the collection of the Library of Congress more or less by chance — as a result of American occupation after World War II.

In 1968 I established the World Political Parties Institute for the express purpose of creating an organization through which political posters could be collected on a regular basis. Political groups are often more responsive when dealing with a formalized institution than with a private individual. The World Political Parties Institute (WPPI) conducts research on political parties and pressure groups of all countries and ideologies. It is located in New York City and corresponds with over 2,000 organizations. Its advisors are political science professors and political campaign consultants. Various aspects of political parties are studied: their histories, their campaigning techniques, and their organizational apparatus. The over-all purpose of WPPI is to analyze the political group

1. France. Students of the Beaux-Arts, Paris. *It's he who is the "chienlit."* Paraphrasing De Gaulle. May, 1968.

2. U.S.S.R. *Press is the powerful weapon of the people.* 1968.

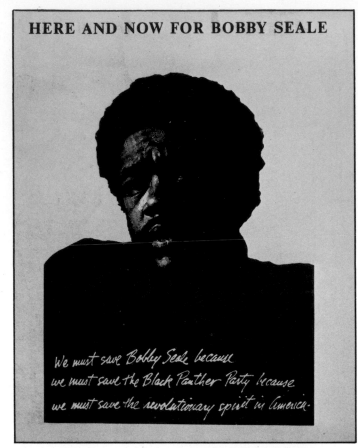

HERE AND NOW FOR BOBBY SEALE

*We must save Bobby Seale because
we must save the Black Panther Party because
we must save the revolutionary spirit in America.*

3. U.S.A. Black Panther Party. 1970.

4.

4, 5. Switzerland. Poster display in Zurich for parliamentary elections. 1971. Poster walls were lent free by the city, with each party allowed one poster per display. Thus the characteristically sober and "rational" Swiss school of graphic design was combined with a "rational," controlled approach to political advertising. Parties participating in the elections included: Labor Party (PdA); Farmer, Trade, and Middle-Class Party (BGP); Christian Democratic People's Party (CVP); Social Democratic Party (SP); Swiss Republican Movement (SRB); Protestant People's Party (EVP); National Action against infiltration of people and fatherland (NA); National Independent Party (LdU); and Liberal Democratic Party (FDP).

5.

as a vehicle for social and economic change. By studying the nature and operation of all parties, WPPI is trying to derive general principles by which parties can be organized and administered. Perhaps the development of such a methodology would lead to a more responsive international political system.

Through an extensive system of contacts in the United States, Europe, and Asia, and also through regular correspondence with political parties and political groups, the WPPI has been able to monitor the poster production activities of many organizations for the last four years. This has contributed in some measure to making the parties aware of the need to preserve their own graphic materials, something few of them had previously considered important. The contacts in foreign countries are usually university students whom I have met during travels abroad.

The propaganda poster collector is truly a rare breed. He is an adventurer, often risking his life to get a poster: propaganda poster collecting already has its own folklore. Posters have been smuggled across politically tense borders. Contacts have removed freshly pasted posters from walls during street fights between students and police. Collectors have entered the heavily guarded headquarters of ultra right- or left-wing revolutionary groups, where they were sometimes mistaken for CIA agents.

Other collectors — of art, film, and advertising posters — have a much safer and more leisurely life.

One of my friends sustained a serious blow during the French student revolt of 1968. While trying to remove a "Le Chienlit, C'est Lui" poster (Fig. 1) from a wall in Paris' Latin Quarter, he was hit in the back of the head by a flying cobblestone and knocked unconscious. He reported that all he could think was "the poster is lost." This is the spirit of the true collector. Luckily, the friend has recuperated and continues his poster collecting functions for WPPI. In the end, he obtained a "Chienlit" poster from an American tourist who was in Paris at the time of the revolt.

Of course, the political collector could reduce the risk by limiting his collection to just one ideological point of view — only Communist posters, for example, or posters of conservative parties. In the real spirit of political poster collecting, however, this is not possible. Each type must be given recognition. Obviously, partisan groups do not always see eye to eye with the collectors; they often cannot understand what the collector sees in the graphics of their opposition. The poster collector must, therefore, avoid alluding to the other parties represented in his collection and give each potential donor the impression that he is only collecting the posters of his persuasion.

Two friends of mine, with large rolls of student posters protesting Soviet occupation, attempted three separate border crossings during the invasion of Czechoslovakia. Each time, the posters were confiscated by border guards. Only the last crossing was successful, although 150 posters still had to be left behind and, one must assume, destroyed. The fear of discovery by a hostile border guard can make anyone regret collecting political posters. Naturally, the collector is anxious to avoid the discovery of controversial matter; in addition, he does not wish to be held up for long explanations or be forced to pay duty. But the fear of confiscation is perhaps the greatest — especially after long hours spent avoiding hostile troops and suspicious students.

Before every border crossing, the decision must be made whether to roll or fold the posters. Rolling, of course, prevents wrinkles, but it also produces a bulkier package. Rolled posters may be explained away as maps, although this is seldom a credible explanation. Folding is a more compact method. Posters can thus be hidden under suitcase linings, between clothing, or in the seat of the pants. But folding effectively mutilates the poster. It leaves creases in the design that will be visible even after ironing or dry-mount pressing.

In August, 1968, one month after the student and labor revolt in France, another friend of WPPI tried to cross the French-Swiss border with 500 Soviet posters he had picked up from a third contact who had arrived from Moscow at the Zurich airport. Rolled up, the posters were lying on the back seat of a Volkswagen. When asked by a French customs officer if he had anything to declare the contact answered "no," but as he drove by the officer noticed the posters and ordered the driver to pull over. The customs officer asked, "What is in the rolls?" "Posters," he was told. The officer grabbed one roll, opened it, and stared at a large picture of Lenin, accompanied by a Russian inscription (Fig. 2). My friend began explaining that these posters

6. West Germany. German Socialist Student Union (SDS). *Everybody talks about the weather. We don't.* 1968.

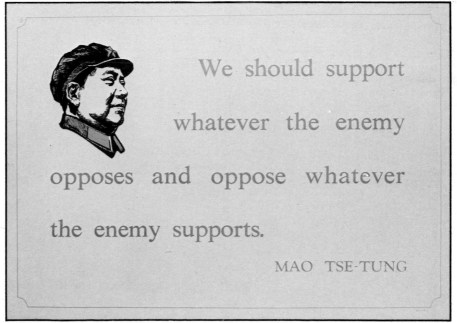

7. China. 1970.

8. Germany (Third Reich). National Socialist Party. *The Marshal and the Corporal fight with us for freedom and equality.*

were collector's items and would be of no use to a French revolution, since they were written in Russian and would be incomprehensible to the average person. The customs people replied that the chief of police must be called in. The contact was ordered to sit down in an office, where he waited three hours for a police chief who never appeared. The officer on duty finally ordered him to cross back into Switzerland, where he could mail the posters to the United States. They could not be brought into France. Relieved that he had not been imprisoned, my friend went to Basel and spent the rest of the day wrapping and mailing posters.

I have seen many good political posters that for various reasons — such as the presence of barbed wire or armed soldiers — I was unable to retrieve. While in Egypt, I discovered a poster of Nasser that had been scribbled over, probably by an Arab distressed by the failure of the war with Israel. The poster was firmly pasted to the wall; I estimated it would require an hour to successfully remove it. As I started the work of detaching it, Arabs gathered around me to watch. "Is this man bold enough to remove a poster of Nasser in broad daylight?" — this is what I suspected the onlookers were thinking. Soon there were shouts of "Israeli spy" from the crowd. The tension became too great, and I was forced to abandon the poster. This is only one of many stories of posters lost forever.

Poster retrieval is an art at which my fellow collectors and I have become quite sophisticated. It requires the collector to assume an air of authority: for instance, he may say that he was told to remove the Bobby Seale poster (Fig. 3) from the walls of the philosophy building at Columbia University. Who authorized him? The Panthers; they need the poster for a table they are setting up in the law school. Lengthy explanations are seldom necessary, but if the collector is prepared with a story while he is removing a poster, he will project an air of confidence and will almost never be stopped. Never let a good political poster pass you by. Don't procrastinate, or you will never have it. Remove it now.

The collector must be bold, assertive, and rational. When approaching a demonstrator in the middle of a parade, he should be polite when asking him for his poster. He should not make the demonstrator stop while arguing with him, but walk along by his side and be sympathetic. The demonstrator's retort that he needs the placard can be answered with the argument that before it is destroyed, it must be saved for posterity; besides, the collector is asking for only one poster; there will be enough left to complete the demonstration.

As you see, it is often through unorthodox tactics that poster collections are made.

About this Book

Prop Art is divided into two sections, an illustrated analysis of various aspects of political poster design and a Gallery of over 800 contemporary posters. It is intended to serve as an introduction to the subject as well as a handbook for the political poster designer. Material on poster design as it relates to propaganda will be found in chapters 1, 3, 4, 5, and 6.

Past books on the poster have tended to take sides; the present volume attempts to be apolitical.

In my opinion, 1967 marks the beginning of increased poster production activity and "poster consciousness." In the Gallery I have therefore reviewed major political events from that time to the present. Of particular interest in this regard are the posters devoted to Vietnam and ecology, the most fertile themes in poster design to emerge in the past few years.

It has taken four years to put this book together. Although it will by no means be the last word on propaganda art, it is my hope that it will stimulate further research and collecting activities.

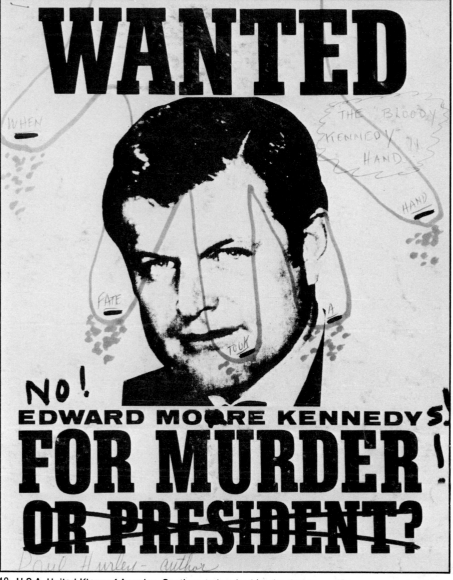

10. U.S.A. United Klans of America. Sentiments inspired by the drowning of a secretary in Edward Kennedy's car, Chappaquiddick, Mass. 1969.

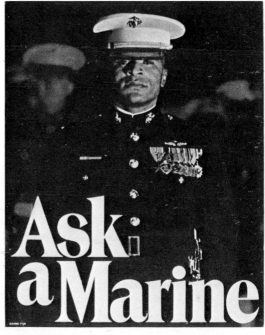

9. U.S.A. U.S. Marine Corps. Recruitment poster. 1970.

11. U.S.A. National Socialist White People's Party. Leaflet. 1967.

the 16th of october

12. U.S.A. Independent Party. Mayoralty election, New York City. Announcement of rally for candidate John Lindsay. 1969.

CHAPTER I
Propaganda Art

Art has been propagandistic since the pharaohs of ancient Egypt. These kings designed their pyramids to project a feeling of power and durability. Similarly, the architecture of the Romans served a political purpose — the glorification of the state. The portraits painted in nineteenth-century France by Jacques-Louis David helped to propagandize an heroic image of Napoleon.

Whether the propaganda content of art reduces its esthetic value is a matter for art historians to debate. The value of art in propaganda is another story; the visual image can help to make abstract political ideas understandable. In posters this usually is done by an association of visual symbols with a textual message. Used exclusively, visual images can suggest allegories, such as Good overcoming Evil, and thus may serve as a universal language. They also help to simplify abstract political theories. Further, if the audience is persuaded to equate (or confuse) the thing represented in design with the actual political reality behind it, poster propaganda has succeeded in both its artistic and its political sense in becoming an effective means of arousal and persuasion.

Over one thousand posters are shown in this book, but they represent a mere sampling of the total volume that has come forth. From a study of these posters, I have attempted to isolate the basic thematic elements and to establish some principles for political poster design to aid both the political artist and the propagandist. Because it is a universal medium, the poster has important characteristics that make it indispensable for any good propagandist's arsenal.

Propaganda in its broadest sense is the systematic spreading — or propagation — of particular ideas, doctrines, and practices. Today the word is often used in a pejorative sense, connoting deception or distortion, but this is not its original meaning.

I have chosen the expression "Prop Art" (propaganda art) to describe the world political poster phenomenon,

13. France. Democratic Union of the Republic (UDR). *Yes to DeGaulle. Yes to France.* 1969.

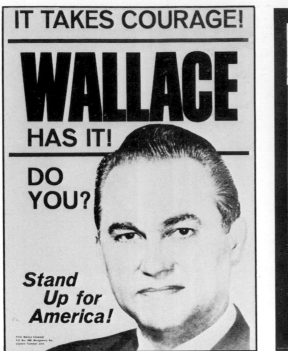

14. U.S.A. Wallace for President Committee. Presidential election. 1968.

15. Lebanon (Palestine guerillas). Front for the Liberation of Palestine. *Shalom and napalm.* 1969.

16. Austria. Communist Party. *Support the world-wide movement: Stop the U.S. bombing of North Vietnam.* 1968.

because "propaganda" best describes these posters. "Political," in its pure sense, means engaged in or taking sides, as in a debate. Many of the posters shown here are more propagandistic than political, because they present an idea without necessarily associating it with a bid for office or a program for reform. Commercial advertising posters are also clearly propagandistic; but they have been excluded as generally having no political content. I have included posters produced by organizations not generally considered political — legal and medical associations, for instance — but which carry on activities to influence public opinion.

This book examines political posters from all over the world, largely those produced since 1967. It testifies to the widespread use of the poster as a means of persuasion.

Poster Propaganda Analysis

My study of poster propaganda does not attempt to determine the validity or logic of the political ideas presented. The techniques are viewed as skills that anyone can acquire and, in the case of politics, that everyone can practice.

Propaganda, when applied to the political poster, means the use of symbols, text, and pictures to influence the attitudes of the audience. Every political group makes propaganda. Indeed, all groups that communicate with mass audiences must be propagandistic.

Because of its abbreviated message and the limited attention span given it by the viewer, the political poster by its nature can be nothing but propagandistic. Rational and extended arguments cannot be communicated through the poster. There is obviously no room on the poster for explanations. Posters containing only text come closest to this; however, they are often so visually undynamic that they fail to attract the viewer's attention in the first place — and so remain unread. Figures 4 and 5 show the highly competitive nature of propaganda graphics.

Propaganda thus has a unique function — the spread of controversial ideas to a broad mass of people. The method is to redefine popular concepts of political and social issues using appropriate visual elements. On the simplest level, if you wish to communicate that your opponent is evil, portray him as a monster. More sophisticated techniques include the rearrangement or reassociation of accepted graphic symbols with other design elements to produce new meanings. The propagandist's task, technically speaking, is to override old symbols, substituting new associations, or to invent wholly new symbols. Later, I shall examine visual styles and problems more extensively.

In general, the revolutionary poster has a more difficult propaganda task than the typical election campaign poster, because it must break up the ascendency of ruling symbols. The revolutionary propagandist must literally create a crisis of conscience by attacking the established symbols and substituting new ones. The reformer or election campaigner, on the other hand, can often maintain the central symbols intact, using familiar images to represent new solutions to old problems.

The propaganda content of posters can be analyzed in terms of the appeals they make. These appeals can be adopted by the effective poster propagandist and used successfully no matter what his political persuasion. Many of the following are so common that they are employed unconsciously. For just this reason, it may be valuable to examine them for what they really are — techniques of manipulation.

Appeal to authority. Here the German Socialist Student Union (SDS) implies that Marx, Lenin, and Engels sanction the reforms proposed by the SDS (Fig. 6). Mao-quotation posters (Fig. 7) are a good example of this type of appeal. The legitimization of Hitler's chancellorship (Fig. 8) by showing him with Marshal Hindenburg is another example.

Sugar-coating. Recruitment posters, among others, do a good deal of sugar-coating in selling the attractiveness of the armed forces (Fig. 9).

Image-making. This applies mainly to the building up of the candidate by projecting a certain style. The use of psychedelic effects in Figure 12 is an attempt to show that the candidate is "with it." Election campaigns are often reduced to a contest of personalities, with issues de-emphasized.

Attack. Instead of dealing with issues, it is often effective to attack the character of the person who makes the argument. This detracts from the real issue and colors it with the candidate's personality. Figure 10 attacks the morality of Kennedy

17. Czechoslovakia. *Why?* Protesting Soviet invasion and occupation. August, 1968.

18. Austria. Freedom Party (FPO). *The Austrian People's Party is without a head. The Socialist Party of Austria brags. But you pay! Vote FPO.* 1968.

THE STREETS OF OUR COUNTRY ARE IN TURMOIL. THE UNIVERSITIES ARE FILLED WITH STUDENTS REBELING AND RIOTING. COMMUNISTS ARE SEEKING TO DESTROY OUR COUNTRY. THE REPUBLIC IS IN DANGER FROM WITHIN AND WITHOUT. WE NEED LAW AND ORDER OR OUR NATION CANNOT SURVIVE...

ADOLPH HITLER 1932

19, 20. U.S.A. These words, attributed to Hitler, have been widely quoted in criticism of the Republican Party's "law and order" platform in the Presidential campaign of 1968. However, scholars have been unable to verify the source of the quote, and it is now doubted that Hitler ever voiced such sentiments.

"The streets of our country are in turmoil. The universities are filled with students rebelling and rioting. Communists are seeking to destroy our country. Russia is threatening us with her might, and the Republic is in danger. Yes—danger from within and without. We need law and order! Without it our nation cannot survive." —Adolph Hitler, 1932

See nr. 19   20.

rather than his political platform. (On this particular poster, the message has been strengthened by a bit of graffiti.)

Appeal to prejudice and special interest. This includes appeals to ethnic or racial prejudice (Fig. 11), nationalism (Fig. 13), and chauvinism (Fig. 14).

Appeal to pity. The common examples of this are pictures of victims of a catastrophe (Figs. 15, 16). The message is that one should take appropriate action to prevent further misery. The exposure of injustice is a related appeal (Fig. 17).

Limiting alternatives. A proposition is placed in front of the audience along with a few black-and-white choices: either the two opposition parties or ours (Fig. 18).

Stolen concept. One uses a concept in a way that changes its antecedent meaning (Figs. 19, 20).

Cliches. In my view, these most commonly occur in the party slogan. At times, a political party will adopt cliches that do not necessarily relate to its program, but that sound smooth enough to be acceptable to all (Fig. 21). "Freedom, Progress, and Security" are catchwords that no one can criticize.

False Cause/Effect ("After this because of this.") Common in much propaganda is the need to establish a cause of failure. The party closest to the problem (such as unemployment) is labeled with the blame, even though it is difficult to establish a causal relationship between its actions and the undesirable results (Fig. 22).

21. Belgium. Socialist Party. *Secure living, future, fortune. Vote Socialist.* 1968.

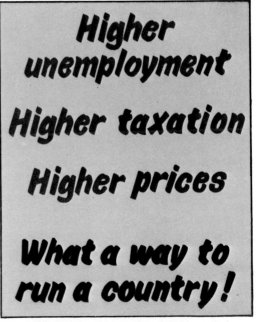

22. Great Britain. Conservative Party. A swipe at the Labour Government. 1968.

CHAPTER II

The International Propaganda Phenomenon

The rationale for a study of the propaganda poster as a world phenomenon has developed as a result of the almost universal use of the poster as a medium of political expression; witness the increasing similarities in election campaign practices of the world's political parties. (The first meeting of the International Association of Campaign Consultants was held in Paris, November 23, 1968. Now consultants from all over the world are provided a forum for the exchange of campaign techniques.) Also new is the appearance of the multi-language political poster produced for export to all parts of the world, most notably by Communist agencies. Additionally, many locally produced political posters have reached world audiences through coverage by international news magazines and television (Fig. 23). Thus, other media pick up the poster's image and project it to a world audience, producing what I term a secondary duplication effect. In some cases, the pictorial poster, bypassing the barriers of language, transmits the only local political information that can be understood by an international audience.

The Poster's Importance Internationally

The popularity and influence of posters varies from country to country for a number of reasons. Some theorists feel that radio and television, particularly in the industrially developed countries, have eroded the poster's importance in the modern election campaign, reducing its role to that of a supplement to other communications media. In addition, there have been environmental pressures on the political poster, mainly in the United States, where there is a movement to abolish posters and billboards from

23. U.S.A. Newspaper photograph of pro-Black Panther demonstration, Columbia University, New York City. 1970.

24. Czechoslovakia. Soviet soldiers tearing down posters protesting Soviet invasion. August, 1968.

25. Czechoslovakia. Czechs replacing protest posters torn down by Soviet soldiers. August, 1968.

26. France. Posters on the Ecole des Beaux-Arts, Paris. 1968.

27. Mexico. Protest poster circulated by students during Olympic Games held in Mexico City in 1968, when eyes of the world were on Mexico.

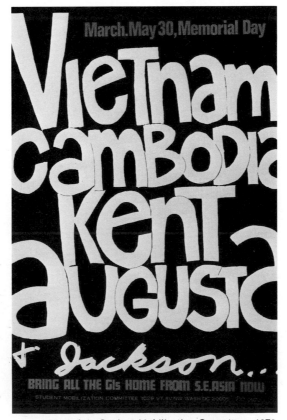

28. U.S.A. Student Mobilization Committee. 1970.

streets and highways as part of the "Keep America beautiful" program. Pressures of this type account to some extent for a phenomenon I shall call the poster-substitute, in which the graphic image of the poster is reproduced on surfaces of varying sizes and shapes. Prominent examples are bumperstickers, buttons, and calendars.

Europe, on the other hand, has a more established tradition of public posting than the United States. In particular, poster kiosks and wall boards on the sides of buildings are an accepted part of the environment. The political poster is assured more display space.

In countries such as China and India, there is no doubt that the poster is particularly important and considerably relied upon. The high illiteracy rate creates a natural audience for this essentially visual medium, and absence of widespread use of television in the Third World generally leaves the political poster in the dominant position as a vehicle for pictorial propaganda. Even in highly industrialized countries, it can be argued that it is easier to avoid television propaganda than a widely distributed political poster.

Television, radio, and sometimes newspapers in many parts of the world are either state controlled, as in France, or subject to easy censorship, as was demonstrated during the Soviet invasion of Czechoslovakia. The poster, however, even in times of political upheavals, often holds its own as a voice of the suppressed opposition. In Czechoslovakia, the posters caricaturing and criticizing the invading troops, seen around the world in newspapers and on television, provided a vivid demonstration of the poster's power and endurance. Although the soldiers tore down many of the posters (Fig. 24), fresh ones appeared every day (Fig. 25).

The cost of television and radio limits the use of these media to relatively wealthy politicians or political bodies. The poster, therefore, remains the most accessible resource for poor and small political groups. The students in France during the May-June uprising (Fig. 26) of 1968 relied heavily — and successfully — on posters. Posters were also used effectively by students in Mexico during the 1968 Summer Olympics (Fig. 27) and in the United States during the student strike protesting the invasion of Cambodia in May of 1970 (Fig. 28).

Political Poster Renaissance

The poster reached a high point as the leading instrument of political persuasion during the two world wars. Posters produced by the British in World War I encouraged patriotism. A Nazi propagandist placed great emphasis on the poster's role in Hitler's rise to power and in the temporary successes of the German war effort in World War II. According to today's poster analysts in the Soviet Union, graphics played a prominent role in the consolidation of power after the Russian Revolution (Fig. 29) and the prosecution of a successful effort in World War II (Fig. 30). The Allies, too, in both world wars, put great stress on poster design and commissioned studies to determine the most effective design techniques for posters (Fig. 31).

The largest volume of propaganda posters today is still produced by the political parties which campaign for election. In fact, this type of poster production has been quite constant since World War II. Significant increases in the total poster volume stem first from distribution by newly created Communist propaganda agencies. These organizations, located in the Arab countries, Cuba, China, and the Soviet Union, produce political posters specially designed for export to other countries. In addition, the political poster, thanks mainly to American business, has also become a "cult" object. It is sold in poster shops and bookstores all over the world (Fig. 32). In fact, the poster no longer needs to find public space. It is purchased and taken into the home to be used as decoration. Many of the cult posters are not sponsored by political organizations; they represent the work of independent artists with strong political feelings. Through caricature, political leaders are often portrayed in foolish and embarrassing situations (President Nixon smoking marijuana with the inscription "Let me make this perfectly clear" [Fig. 33]; or Vice-President Agnew depicted as a strong man strangling the Statue of Liberty [Fig. 34]). These cult items have for the most part been published by political liberals and leftist artists, but the right wing has also begun participating in the poster cult. As an example, the Ku Klux Klan produced a full-color poster of their Imperial Wizard, Robert M. Sheldon, wearing his robes with a cross burning in the

29. U.S.S.R. *Our strength will not subside.* 1917.

30. U.S.S.R. *For the mother country.* 1943.

31. Great Britain. Recruitment poster, World War I.

32. U.S.A. Marboro Bookstore, New York City.

34. U.S.A. Barra Productions. Vice-President Agnew. 1970.

33. U.S.A. Barra Productions. President Nixon. 1970.

background (Fig. 35). This poster has been sold throughout the South by a mail-order advertisement in *The Fiery Cross,* the official Klan magazine. The right wing, however, has found few nationwide distributors willing to sell its cult objects.

Thus, we can legitimately speak of a poster renaissance — a return to the great popularity of posters that was evident during the two world wars. The renaissance has been sparked during the last five years by the May-June riots in Paris (1968) and the Cultural Revolution in China, and assisted by increased facilities for production and distribution and a new poster consciousness fostered by merchants.

The International Political Spectrum

Some general observations will help explain our placement of political and propaganda groups in the various positions of the international political spectrum, which may be visualized as a horseshoe with the extreme rightists at one end and the extreme leftists at the other. As with any categorizations, there will be disagreements; some parties are borderline, and some are perhaps conservative on some issues, liberal on others. But placing them on a spectrum will give us a general notion of their platforms; it will also make clear which parties are ideological neighbors. Up to now, propaganda posters have represented a vast amorphous phenomenon. Locating them on the spectrum gives us tools with which to analyze this phenomenon.

I shall use the labels left and right when referring to various parties and the posters they produce. I have not sought fine distinctions here, but basic ideological slants. This will become particularly significant in my discussion of poster design and symbology.

35. U.S.A. United Klans of America. Robert M. Sheldon, Imperial Wizard. 1969.

36. Germany. *For the war loan!* World War I.

37. France. *We'll get them! The second loan for national defense. Subscribe.* World War I.

CHAPTER III
Poster Literature

Before looking at the types, functions, psychology, and graphic elements of political posters, let us survey what has already been written about them.

Poster-analytic literature is a body of writing describing the elements that go into the effective political poster. It consists of magazine articles, party pamphlets, and a few books devoted to the history and art of the poster. The literature, like posters themselves, comes from many parts of the world; and particularly from the Soviet Union, Germany, Austria, the United States, France, and Cuba. Most poster analysis is written from a partisan point of view; that is, the writer reflects his own political prejudices in deciding which posters are designed well and which poorly. Extremist and moderate parties traditionally have opposing views on what constitutes effective poster design.

Partisan analysis is often encountered in Soviet publications on the political poster. Demosfenova, in *Sovetski Politicheski Plakat (The Soviet Political Poster),* refers to the poster as an instrument for mobilizing the people for revolutionary struggles around the world and asserts its uselessness and drabness in election campaigns of the bourgeois parties. Giving the view of the moderate parties, Horst Reiman, in *Wahlplakate (Campaign Posters),* a study of West German election posters since the end of World War II, says that election poster design should adopt a "rational and honest" approach. He maintains that, by contrast, the poster art of the National Socialists and the Communists is "irrational and too emotional."

Design books, in general, imply that the political poster is somehow unique, while frequently prescribing techniques similar to those used for designing commercial and advertising posters. These techniques are usually simplistic. Ivanov's *Kak Sozdaetsya Plakat (How to Design a Poster)* and Arno Scholz's *Das Einmaleins der Politische Werbung (The One-Times-One Table of Political Advertising)* consider simplicity and clarity as watchwords for the political poster. Scholz outlines a check list of nine points to consider in designing any political poster. These points are representative of design principles set forth in almost every party manual or mimeograph on political campaigning:

1. Put as little as possible on the poster (design or text).
2. Arrange the design and lettering to attract the passer-by's attention.
3. Consider where the poster will be hung or displayed.
4. Consider how effective it will look next to other political posters.
5. Text and design large enough they can be seen from a prescribed distance, usually 30 to 45 feet.
6. Use harmonious color combinations.
7. Design and text must complement each other.
8. Use a modern art style.
9. The design should not detract from the impact of the words.

The Analytical Approaches

Psychological Studies

Some studies have attempted to go beyond mere design techniques to explore the psychological impact of the political poster. I have come across four major poster studies that are psychologically oriented.

Erwin Schockel's *Das Politische Plakat: Eine psychologische Betrachtung (The Political Poster: A Psychological Study),* published in 1939, was an official Nazi propaganda manual. Although his study is admittedly intuitive and partisan, it is the classical work on the political poster. Neither before nor since has there been a more comprehensive attempt at political poster analysis. Schockel's book contains 300 pages of photographs and text devoted exclusively to political poster design. In the present work I have sought to imitate his comprehensiveness, but I have had the freedom to be more neutral in presenting the principles of political poster design.

Schockel's book looks at posters from the First and Second World Wars and describes them as being "good" or "bad" in design. As an example, Schockel identifies Germany's World War I war loan (Fig. 36) and recruiting

38. Great Britain. World War I.

39. U.S.A. *Enlist U.S. Army*. World War I.

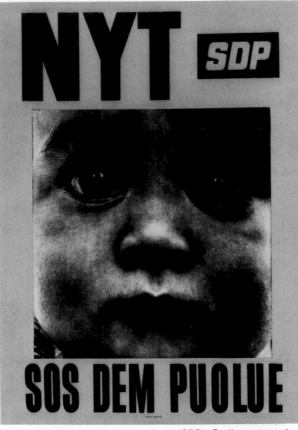

40. Finland. Social Democratic Party (SDP). Parliamentary elections. *Now: SDP.* 1966.

41. U.S.A. 1970.

posters as bad design. Those of France (Fig. 37), Great Britain (Fig. 38), and the U.S. (Fig. 39) on the same subject are pronounced good. He then proceeds to show how Nazi poster art was an improvement over the German posters produced previously. In addition, he makes the usual attacks on the decadence of the art forms used in the opponent's posters.

Schockel speaks of the political poster in grandiose terms. As an example, he considers that Hitler's rapid rise to power is attributable to effectively designed posters. He also asserts that the Germans lost World War I because of the inferiority of their war loan and recruiting posters. He argues that the posters failed to inspire a national war effort because of their lackluster design.

Young and Rubicam's *Study of Canadian War Posters,* compiled in 1942, is based on a survey of Canadian war posters, compiled for the National Advisory Council on Government Posters of the Graphics Division, Office of Facts and Figures, Washington, D.C. The study recommends how to effectively design recruiting and war loan posters. In an attempt to pick out the most effective posters and to describe their characteristics, 403 case studies of Canadians' reactions to their war posters were made.

Art as Propaganda, With Emphasis on Iconographic Aspects, 1956, is Edward Janicik's master's thesis for the University of Pittsburgh. This study reflected the increasing concern by Americans with the so-called psychological threat of propaganda, which grew out of its widespread use in World War II and also in the Korean War. Janicik's thesis attempts to relate the art mode of graphic design to the particular psychological effect desired.

Lastly, the PLANT Approach (Perception/Precinct Level Attitude-Normative Technique) was described to the author in a series of interviews with John d'Arc Lorenz of Cyr, Picard & Associates, Washington, D.C. This approach represents perhaps the most scientific attempt at analyzing and designing posters to date. Cyr, Picard is one of the increasing number of small campaign consulting firms run by psychologists and specialists in political science. PLANT is a technique of measuring the attitudes of the prospective audience through psychoanalytic tests, and translating these results into design and word symbols. The test data, along with color possibilities also gleaned from testing, are

42. France. Communist Party. *Fight the voraciousness of the capital-ist monopolies that are ruining France. Support the Communist Party, party of the working class, the people and the nation.* 1970.

43. U.S.A. Poster based on a widely circulated newspaper photograph of Kent State killings, with announcement of student rally inked in at the top. 1970.

44. U.S.A. 1970.

45. Great Britain. Liberal Party. (Jeremy Thorpe is leader of the Liberal Party.) 1970.

then used to evolve guidelines for the poster designs. Because of the unique nature of this attempt at political poster design, PLANT will be treated in a separate chapter.

Sociological Analysis

Posters used in demonstrations by students and workers throughout the world have been reproduced in books as documents of recent political events. An example is Louis F. Peters' *Kunst und Revolte, Das Politische Plakat und der Aufstand der franzoesischen Studenten (Art and Revolt: The Political Poster and the French Student Rebellion).* Having spent the duration of the May-June uprising of 1968 in Paris, Peters observed at first hand the "team concept" employed in the production of over 300 different political posters, printed in average editions of three hundred by the students of the Ecole des Beaux-Arts. His observations are relevant for smaller political organizations that rely heavily on the poster for their propaganda activities. The same techniques were reported used in Czechoslovakia, Mexico, and the United States by student groups.

Recently, Susan Sontag wrote an introductory essay to *The Art of Revolution* in which she analyzed the poster from a politico-social perspective. Miss Sontag contends that posters could not exist before the historic conditions of modern capitalism, and that the advent of the poster reflects the development of an industrialized economy whose goal is ever-increasing mass consumption. The rise of the poster, she says, parallels the development of the modern secular, centralized nation-state, with its rhetoric of mass political participation. Miss Sontag sees the analysts' insistence that the poster's major function is persuasion as deriving from their own cultural milieu. As an example, she says the stress placed on the poster's "selling function" — that is, the promoting of candidates and party platforms — is related to the society's mercantile context.

Magazine Articles

The other types of poster-analytical literature are less easy to classify because they are fragmented. Typical are the articles found in art and political magazines that review the newest developments in poster art, but they make only passing references to effective design techniques. Dugald Stermer's "The Agit Pop Art of Cuba" *(Ramparts,* 1968), and Genevieve Morel's "Poster Politics in Red China" (*Réalités*, 1968) are examples. This also includes my own article, "Prop Art" (*Print*, 1969). In addition, there are art books dealing with the posters that discuss political posters only in terms of their artistic aspects.

The Poster Message

The analysts do not agree about the nature of the poster's appeal nor how this appeal should be made. Although they have probably never faced each other in actual debate, I have attempted here to juxtapose their differing viewpoints.

Rational Versus Emotional Appeals

Should a poster be rational or emotional in its appeal? Adolf Hitler, in *Mein Kampf*, pointed out that the specific function of the political posters "is in attracting the attention of the crowd, not in educating those who are already educated or who are striving for education and knowledge. Its effect for the most part must be aimed at the emotions, and only in a limited way at the so-called intellect." Horst Reiman proposes the opposite approach for campaign posters, insisting that election campaign posters should appeal to reason rather than emotions. High-pitched slogans and fiery symbols should be replaced by a "more reserved, truthful, honestly engaged, convincing, and moderate appeal."

The most effective method of poster design would certainly vary the appeal according to the desired goal. Parties campaigning for office have certainly been known to use emotional posters (Figs. 40, 42). And extremist parties with little hope of election victory have criticized their opposition with emotional arguments rather than rational ones.

A symbolic illustration of rationality in the campaign poster was the appeal to a reasonable choice embodied in the "owl motif" of Switzerland's Liberal party used in the 1968 parliamentary elections. A series of posters depicting such slogans as "Be wise with your ballot, vote Liberal" showed owls with human faces (Fig. 50).

The question of whether the poster should appeal to the emotions or to reason is also reflected in the analysis of the war posters. Young and Rubicam's study concluded that the war loan and recruiting posters must be emotional rather than rational in their appeal. The 403 case studies revealed that people were more moved to

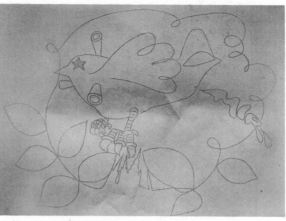

47. Czechoslovakia. *Peace*. Protesting Soviet invasion. August, 1968.

46. France. Democratic Union of the Republic (UDR). *Participation UDR*. 1969.

48. U.S.A. Student Mobilization Committee. 1970.

49. U.S.A. World War I.

50. Switzerland. Liberal Party. *When others sleep*...Artist: Celestino Piatti. 1968.

support the war effort by emotion than reason.

Pressure groups tend to concentrate on emotional appeals. They are usually promoting one issue and seek to get an idea across rather than to create a consensus of opinion among diverse groups. Their singlemindedness inspires fervor or emotionality in the things they say.

The concepts of "rational" and "emotional," as used by the traditional analysts, are too simplistic for today's competitive propagandist or campaign consultant. Likewise, the motto "keep the poster simple" is quite unsophisticated when compared to Lorenz's PLANT approach.

Figurative Versus Non-Figurative Posters

The analysts disagree as to whether the political poster is more effective as an abstract (non-figurative) or a pictorial (figurative) design. Young and Rubicam concluded from their research that abstract war posters "are likely to be misunderstood or not understood at all." Scholz and Lorenz both suggest simple abstractions, where only a few lines and a symbol are used, and not the complexities ordinarily associated with abstract art. Lorenz believes that there is more chance that the viewer of an abstract design will relate favorably to the poster's message if he has a positive attitude toward the poster's two basic design elements: line and color. He says that certain colors and angles of lines can be used to influence the viewer's attitudes favorably or unfavorably. These will be discussed in more detail in Chapter 5.

Some analysts also argue that the figurative design tends to limit the political argument because of its specificity. Thus, the poster designer will exclude a large potential audience if he does not choose graphic images, those that will be understood by all. The poster designer may find it difficult to select a photograph or representative form that will appeal to a very broad group. Schockel's solution to this problem is very similar to Lorenz's, although Schockel continued to accept figurative designs; he stipulated, however, that they be "clear, simple, and sometimes even primitive to be successful." Some figurative posters, using the photograph or photo-collage, have special advantages of their own. Schockel praises the photographic poster for its conveyance of the "truth": "The observer cannot help but believe that he has

51. U.S.S.R. *Have* you *signed up?* World War I.

52. U.S.A. U.S. Marine Corps. Recruitment poster. 1970.

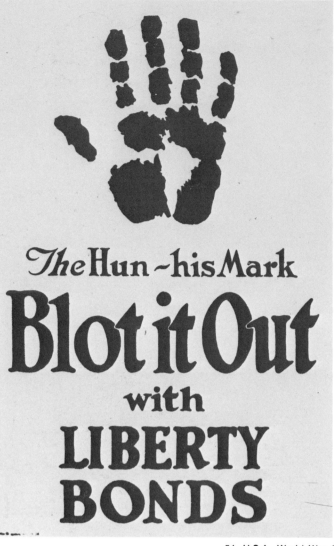

The Hun ~ his Mark

Blot it Out

with

LIBERTY BONDS

54. U.S.A. World War I.

the truth before him, since a photograph cannot lie." Today this type of poster is still widely used. Palestine liberation groups employed photographs of refugees as proof of the "need for guerilla warfare against Israel" (Fig. 41). Another example is the photograph of the Kent State shooting of a college student (Fig. 43). A similar treatment was given to the poster showing a black student shot by the police in Augusta, Georgia, in 1970 (Fig. 44).

As we have seen, poster literature to a large extent is highly biased. In the next chapters, I shall attempt to sift neutral principles from it — principles that can be applied to all groups, no matter what their position on the political spectrum. It is hoped in this way that the reader, no matter who he is, will be helped in designing effective posters.

Today, most political campaign consultants around the world operate on the same intuitive basis as the poster analysts. The lack of a great number of experienced poster designers who can rely on tutored intuition makes it imperative that scientific testing techniques be developed by political groups. Polling methods have been used by campaign consultants in other areas, such as measuring attitudes on political issues, but they still await application to political graphic design.

53. South Vietnam. *"Open arms" policy is the only way of escape.* A call for support for the Saigon government.

CHAPTER IV

Poster Types and Functions

The Poster as an Effective Medium

The poster has unique qualities which distinguish it from other media. First, unlike television or radio, the poster can leave a lasting image. In *Kunst und Revolte,* Peters concludes that instead of competing with the poster, television has given new importance to it by making man less print-conscious and more picture-conscious than ever before. In Peters' words, "television and cinema have heightened man's pictorial experience so that the printed word in politics has become secondary to the poster." Second, the poster is also one of the cheapest media, so it is accessible to small political groups and is thus an ideal vehicle for experimenting and risk-taking as well. Obtaining wooden frames, nails, silkscreen, paint and paper does not involve great expense. And, in addition to having a potential for large circulation, the poster can penetrate areas other media might not reach. Finally, the poster image is relatively durable. It permits the viewer great latitude in interpreting and understanding the message. He can look at his own pace. On the other hand, television and radio set the time and pace at which audiences must view or listen. Here the medium is controlling, and the audience is passive.

Schockel summed up the poster's advantages vis-à-vis other media: "The printed word can go unread, the radio can be turned off, the political meeting does not have to be attended, but the political poster cannot be avoided. Only the blind, the bedridden, and the prisoner cannot come into contact with the poster."

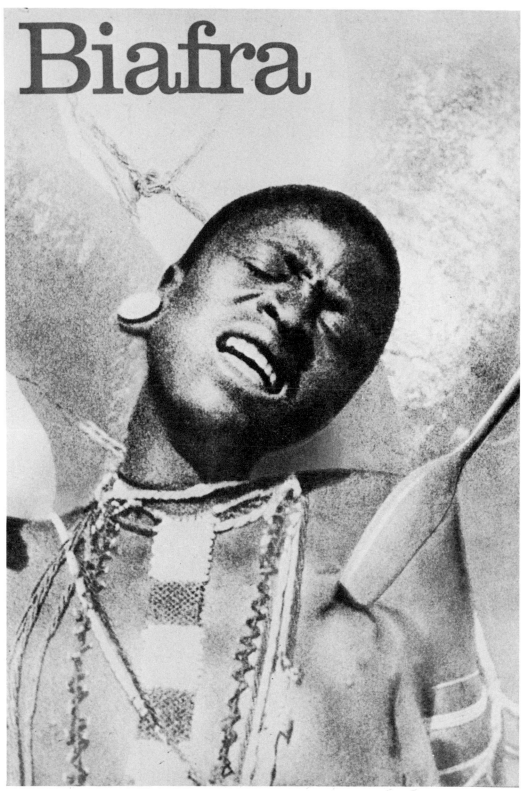

55. Caritas (Catholic charity in Europe). 1968.

U.S. Imperialism, Get Out of South Viet Nam!
L'impérialisme américain hors du Sud-Vietnam!
¡Fuera el imperialismo norteamericano del Sur de Vietnam!

57. China. *U.S. Imperialists get out of South Vietnam.*

Poster Types

One may classify posters in various ways. My classification relates the poster to its producer or sponsor. An alternative method would be classification by theme: protest, revolution, recruitment, war loan, election campaign, announcements, social education, and so forth. But such a classification system is too loose, since many posters would fall into more than one category, depending upon the viewer's perspective. As an example, one can debate whether a poster of a political candidate calling for U.S. withdrawal from Vietnam is an election campaign or protest poster. Likewise, whether a poster is protesting an injustice or making a call for revolution is a distinction that even its producers might not draw. However, the organization that produced the poster can always be identified.

The four major poster producers are political parties, pressure groups, governments, and private sponsors.

Political Party Posters

Election campaign posters comprise the great bulk of posters produced every year throughout the world. They are mainly used for two purposes: to identify the candidate and his party to the electorate (name recognition) (Fig. 45); and to identify the campaign promises with the party or candidate (issue/slogan identification) (Fig. 46). Most political parties produce campaign posters at local,

56. U.S.S.R. *Racist assassins are answerable!* 1909.

58. Cuba. OSPAAAL.

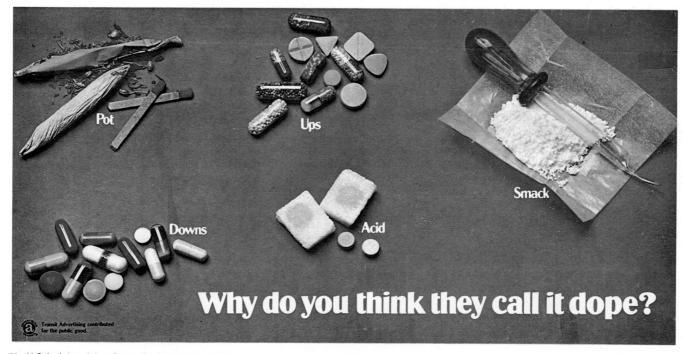

59. U.S.A. Advertising Council of America. 1971.

37

60. Nationalist China. *Cultivate habits of cleanliness and obey the rules of environmental sanitation.*

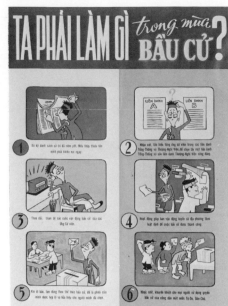

62. South Vietnam. *What do you do during elections?* Illustrated explanation of voting procedures. 1967.

61. South Korea. *June 25, 1950: The Korean War broke out, with the Communist North Korean troops invading the Republic of Korea.*

regional, and national levels. Some parties, such as Sarawak's National Party, have reported to the WPPI that they do not believe in the effectiveness of the poster.

Pressure Group Posters

Pressure groups usually promote a single issue or program. Pressure groups include the anti-war groups, environmental action groups, women's lib, and the Ku Klux Klan. They are often short-lived and do not appeal to a broad mass of people; hence their slogans can be inflammatory, and their posters can be radically designed. Today, ecologists form the most active pressure groups producing posters.

Pressure groups produce posters both spontaneously and in more calculated manners. Posters hastily drawn by the students in Prague as Soviet troops were invading (Fig. 47), and the more carefully planned efforts of the Student Mobilization Committee to End the War in Vietnam (Fig. 48) characterize the two types.

Government-Sponsored Posters

Government-sponsored war posters include: posters to recruit volunteers for the military, prevalent during the two world wars (Figs. 49, 51), and since (Fig. 52); posters to encourage the enemy to defect (now being used by the South Vietnamese government against the Viet Cong [Fig. 53]); posters to raise money through the purchase of war bonds (Fig. 54) or through relief contributions (recently inspired in the United States and Europe by the situation in Biafra [Fig. 55]).

Government-sponsored posters for external propaganda, particularly prevalent in the socialist countries, are produced by special government agencies, some of which are involved in a continuous ideological commentary on world events through political posters. Shown here are examples from the Soviet Union (Fig. 56), China (Fig. 57), and Cuba (Fig. 58). The United States does not produce posters for external influence.

Finally, some governments sponsor posters for internal propaganda — political and social education of their people. Topics include drug abuse (Fig. 59); health (Fig. 60); and celebration of national holidays (Fig. 61). Recently the South Vietnamese government issued posters explaining the election procedure (Fig. 62). Many seemingly neutral subjects are often slanted to meet the ideological requirements of the political party in power.

Privately-Sponsored Posters

This category is comprised mainly of posters generated by what I shall refer to as the "pop-industrial complex" (inspired by the military-industrial complex). In the last five years, the poster (including the political poster) has become a commercial art item sold in bookstores and specialty poster shops. These shops also sell other kinds of paraphernalia, such as peace buttons, dart boards with political candidates' pictures on them, and so forth. A loose alliance of artists, craftsmen, and entrepreneurs has grown out of this commercial enterprise. I call it pop-industrial because it mainly involves the marketing of commercial art. The political aspect of this market activity focuses on the poster criticizing the established order, financed and distributed by a network of producers and shops (the complex). Two prominent operations of this type are the world-wide affiliates of Personality Posters, Inc., and America's largest mail order distributor Marboro Books, both based in New York City. This area is so prolific that posters produced by the pop-industrial complex are found throughout the Gallery. Many of the posters produced by political parties and pressure groups are sold through this new marketing apparatus (Fig. 63) or are jointly financed by the pressure group and poster entrepreneurs. In posters made for sale, political messages often are phrased like commercial advertisements (Fig. 64). The propaganda impact is probably greatest on the teenage generation, which is the chief purchaser. Private sponsorship also includes corporations that carry on public service advertising as an adjunct to the direct selling of their products.

Poster Functions

Persuasion

Political posters aim to persuade in very specific ways. They may seek broad support for a platform (Fig. 65) or focus all attention on a candidate. When an audience has been selected, a tailor-made appeal is directed to it. During election campaigns, appeals are commonly made to youth (Fig. 66); the family (Fig. 67); women (Fig. 68); workers (Fig. 69); and the aged (Fig. 70). In protest and propaganda campaigns, the segmented audiences

63. U.S.A. The New Mobilization Committee to End the War in Vietnam. Based on a pen and-ink drawing of Picasso. 1969.

64. U.S.A. 1969.

65. Great Britain. Labour Party.

66. Finland. Liberal Party. *A change for the better.*

67. Italy. Christian Democratic Party (DC). *The Family: Let's vote DC.*

68. Australia. Labor Party.

69. Austria. Peoples Party (OVP). *We have full employment and a stable currency. The Socialists want to change this.* 1969.

70. Canada. New Democratic Party. 1968.

include women (Fig. 71) and blacks (Fig. 72).

As an ideological weapon, the poster should seek to gain broad support by minimizing ideological arguments, appealing to attitudes, and concentrating on specific issues. The audience for any political poster can be defined three ways: the opponents, the sympathizers, and the uncommitted. The formula is first to appeal to the uncommitted, second to blunt the impact of the opponents' arguments, and, finally, to reinforce recognized support.

Dissenters to the view that persuasion is the political poster's primary goal insist that its main purpose is to serve a cultural function. Peters sees the political poster in the context of a world-wide cultural revolution, which has had its main impact so far in Communist China and France. He believes that "posters, good posters at any rate, cannot be considered mainly as instruments for communicating something whose normative form is 'information.' . . . What is recognized as an *effective* poster is one that transcends its utility in delivering [a] message. . . . Through posters, art is becoming democratized."

Posters that are designed to announce, to inform, to criticize, to satirize, to commemorate, and to raise money, may also contain strong elements of persuasion. Schockel points out the obvious fact that a poster announcing a party meeting, in addition to being informative, should also seek to persuade people to come to that meeting. Indeed, Schockel points out that the political poster can serve many functions, but that its overriding concern should be persuasion. Likewise, satire or criticism of the opposition in a cartoon-poster is pointless unless it reflects well on the sponsoring party.

Commemoration

Commemoration posters are widely produced. President Nixon's visit to Italy in 1969 inspired the Christian Democratic Party to produce a poster honoring him (Fig. 73). The same thing occurred when President Johnson visited South Korea in 1967 (Fig. 74).

Communist parties in the last three years have produced many posters celebrating events and people in the world-wide Communist movement. The one-hundredth anniversary of Lenin's birthday was celebrated in France (Fig. 75) and Madagascar (Fig. 76), among other countries.

Artists in the Soviet Union were mobilized to express their graphic sentiments about the fiftieth year of the Communist Revolution (Fig. 77). In 1969, the satellite countries of the Soviet Union, such as Rumania, celebrated various socialist birthdays as well as their respective liberations from fascism by the U.S.S.R.

Pressure groups have a unique way of commemorating events. Even though these groups are sometimes relatively short-lived, they quickly begin to cultivate a traditionalist aura through use of the political poster. Good examples are the commemoration of student martyrs of the various rebellions, for instance, in France (Fig. 78) and in the United States (Fig. 79).

Announcements

Besides persuading people to think certain ways about political and social issues, the poster has the practical function of acting as the "herald" for the political meeting. Whether large or small, many groups use only posters to make their supporters aware of these "congregations of the faithful."

Among the most interesting announcement posters of recent years are those publicizing poster exhibitions (Fig. 80). These exhibitions serve two purposes: to sell original poster art as part of a fund-raising campaign; and to satisfy public curiosity about current events. An example of the latter was a Cuban poster exhibition held in Paris in 1970 on the theme of the Vietnam War (Fig. 81). The Italian Republican Party produces political posters advertising current-events exhibitions, especially in the scientific area. These give the party a progressive or public service (Fig. 82).

Fund-Raising

Most recently, the poster has been used as an aid in raising funds. Posters especially conceived as collector's items have been offered for sale to students and art enthusiasts. Such posters were produced and sold by the McCarthy Campaign Committee (Fig. 83) and by American anti-war groups, such as the Student Mobilization Committee To End The War in Vietnam (SMC) (Fig. 84) and the Fifth Avenue Peace Parade Committee (Fig. 85).

Functions can, of course, be combined. The Cesar Chavez poster (Fig. 88) served both as an announcement of a benefit and as a collector's

71. U.S.A. Black Panther Party. Announcement of rally to release six Black Panther women from prison. 1969

72. U.S.A. Socialist Workers Party. 1970.

73. Italy. Christian Democratic Party. *The Christian Democrats salute President Nixon, reaffirming the bonds of friendship and solidarity of the Italian people with the people of the United States, in the pledge for peace and liberty. 1969.*

74. South Korea. Democratic Republican Party. *Welcome Johnson.* 1967.

75. France. Communist Party. Announcement of meeting to celebrate Lenin centennial. 1970.

76. Madagascar. Announcement of meeting to celebrate Lenin centennial. 1970.

77. U.S.S.R. *Time works toward Communism.* 1967.

78. France. Students. *To the middle class: You haven't understood anything.* 1968.

item whose sale would raise money for the California grape pickers.

Satire/Criticism

While the persuasive poster is generally positive (Fig. 86), the critical poster concentrates on exposure, attacking greed (Fig. 87) or failure, for example. Visual devices sometimes lend special flavor to these posters. Two posters illustrating smear techniques (Fig. 89, 90) actually use the smear as a graphic element. The use of caricature (satire) will be further discussed in Chapter 5, under mode of presentation.

80. U.S.A. National Welfare Rights Organization (NWRO). Announcement of art auction. Artist: Leonard Baskin 1970.

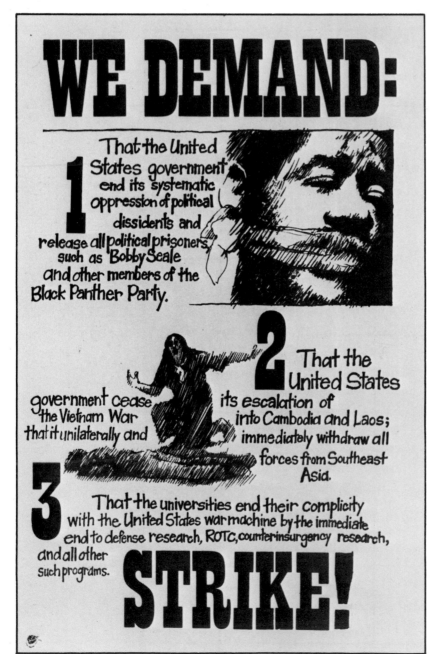

79. U.S.A. Student poster urging strike. 1970.

81. France. Announcement of Cuban poster exhibition. 1970.

82. Italy. Republican Party. *Do we need a department for scientific research?* Exhibition announcement. 1968.

84. U.S.A. Student Mobilization Committee to End the War in Vietnam. 1970.

83. U.S.A. Health Professions for McCarthy. Eugene McCarthy campaigning for the Democratic Presidential nomination. Artist: Ben Shahn. 1968.

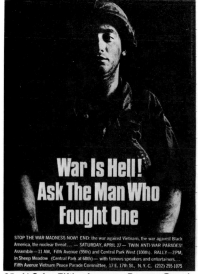

85. U.S.A. Fifth Avenue Peace Parade Committee. 1970.

86. New Guyana. Peoples Progressive Party. 1968.

87. Belgium. United Peoples Party. *PVV (Party for Freedom and Progress) is a pest for Vlaanderen (Northern part of Belgium). Flemish interest is our interest.* 1968.

88. U.S.A. National Farm Workers Service Center. 1968.

CHAPTER V

Basic Elements of Political Graphic Design

To produce an effective political poster, one has to master more than basic design principles of simplicity, clarity, balance, emphasis, unity, and attention-getting. These elements are necessary, but the techniques of design for the political poster also involve complex choices of art style, mode of presentation, and symbolic representation.

Subjectivity of Poster Design Guidelines

Most approaches to effective design are subjective and based on the artist's or propagandist's intuition. Schockel devoted an entire chapter of his book to the analysis of what he considered good and bad political posters. But in Schockel's case, they were judged to be effective because they were produced by the winning side. One of Schockel's main points in *Das Politische Plakat* was that the poster design of the Allies in the First World War was more effective because they won the war.

Another of Schockel's criteria for good and bad political posters was the designer's race: if the poster was designed by a Jew, chances are that it was ineffective — "Jews are corrupt and incapable of good graphic design." Schockel claims that the poster in Figure 91 is an example of Jewish corruption because it depicts an incorrect defense position. In Schockel's words, "the Jew could not deny his race. Where in the world is there a strongman who would not think of pushing away his attacker, but the Jew who made this poster did not think of this." Ironically, one of the most powerful German posters of this period (because it was noticed, remembered, and inspired action) was designed by John Hearthfield for the Communist Party (Fig. 92). Hearthfield was a Jew.

89. Austria. Communist and Left Socialist Parties. *Against the OVP (People's Party) and the FPO (Freedom Party). Vote Communist and Left Socialist.* 1968.

90. Belgium. United People's Party. *"Zwartberg (coal mine riot): BSP (Belgian Socialist Party). Work, welfare: United People's Party."* 1968.

91. Germany. Frei Korps. *Protest against the theft of the German* Saarland.

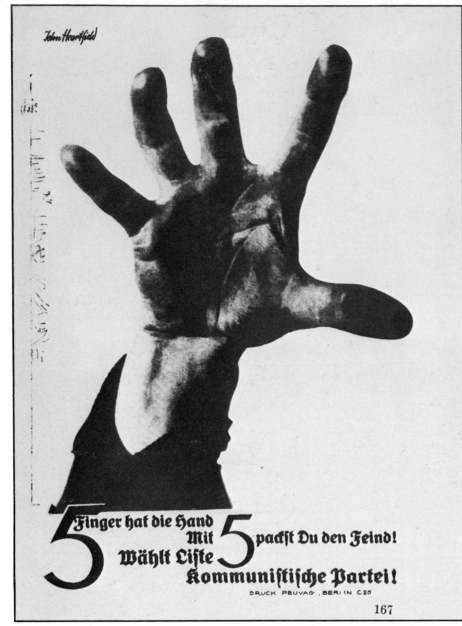

92. Germany (Third Reich). Communist Party. *5 fingers has a hand. With these 5 grab the enemy.* Artist: John Hearthfield.

Schockel makes a valid point when he criticizes German poster design during the First World War as being inferior to British and French designs. The latter were more persuasive and helped to mobilize the war effort. A French recruitment poster (Fig. 37) is called effective by Schockel because "it expressed an almost religious enthusiasm, nourished with the thought of possible revenge." The British poster "Feed the Guns" is successful, according to Schockel, because "it is purely directed toward the reaching of the goal and shows simply and clearly the sacrifices that must be made in order to obtain victory."

German posters of World War I are considered inferior examples of poster design because they fail to arouse any strong emotions in the viewer (Fig. 93). But Schockel cites the German posters produced by Mjoelner (Franz Schweizer) as representative of good Nazi poster design (Figs. 94, 95). To demonstrate this, he shows two different uses of the fist to illustrate effective design techniques. The first, the German Communist version (Fig. 96), is the inferior design, because the fist hovering over the table appears weak. In the second design (Fig. 97), executed by Mjoelner, the fist crashes down on the table. This, Schockel concludes, is a strong rendering of the idea of "threat." In general Schockel seems to have an intuitive grasp of what constitutes effective poster design, but he is unable to express this in non-subjective terms.

The Art Style of the Political Poster

Contemporary art movements play an important role in influencing the political poster designer. One of Scholz's basic rules for the poster is that "the most modern art style should be employed." Schockel is not as flexible in his guidelines for style. Like most ideologists, Schockel believed the art style of the political poster should reflect the attitude of the party toward art.

Today, only the Soviets and Communist Chinese seem to exhibit a uniform art style — socialist realism — in their posters. Genevieve Morel, in her article "Poster Politics in Red China," reports that there are signs that the influence of socialist realism is on the wane in China and something that can be reasonably called

93. Germany. War loan announcement. World War I.

96. Germany (Third Reich). Communist Party (KPD). *An end to the system. KPD—Row 3.*

97. Germany. (Third Reich). National Socialist Party. *An end to this corruption. Vote National Socialist—Row 4.*

a "modern" Chinese style — actually a reversion to classicism — is now trying to emerge. This can be seen by comparing the completely different renditions of the Red Army soldier in 1967 (Fig. 98) — realist — and in 1968 (Fig. 99) — classical. The new Chinese posters display not only a classical art style but also a classic literary tradition (Figs. 100, 101). In trying to break away from the Soviet influence (Fig. 102), the Chinese, instead of encouraging the emergence or adoption of new art forms, as was done in Cuba, have reverted to traditional forms, giving them suitable ideological content. The pre-Revolution Chinese art depicted human beings in a decorative fashion. After the Revolution, Communists encouraged the artists to emulate socialist realism, which had the effect of stultifying the development of their art.

But the reversion to classical imagery may only represent a period of "rest and recuperation" for poster art, following the strains imposed on it by the Cultural Revolution, when the Red Guards (Fig. 103), the army, and the peasants (Fig. 104) were the dominant concern and therefore the dominant poster theme. Mao Tse-tung is less emphasized in these newer, or classical, posters than in the posters that appeared during the Cultural Revolution. Then his image was everywhere (Fig. 105), even as part of the sun (Fig. 106), shown shining on oceans of Chinese peoples.

By contrast, Nationalist China approaches poster design in a much more subdued fashion. Little attention is given to figurative posters. With the textual poster, a more rational tone is presented (Figs. 107, 108). However, such slogans as "Invade the Mainland" are too emotional for the weak graphic presentation they are given. They clearly need more pictorial content to be effective.

Most art styles — Pop art, Op art, Art Nouveau, psychedelic art, as well as the techniques of commercial advertising art — have been adopted by political parties or pressure groups to sell their messages and their candidates. The Communist Party of Cuba, less orthodox than those of Communist China or the Soviet Union, uses Pop art styles in its posters (Fig. 109). The Republican Party of Italy did a series of posters for the 1968 elections using Op art designs (Fig. 110). The Black Panthers also produced a poster using a minor Op art effect (Fig. 111). The willingness of

94. Germany (Third Reich). National Socialist Party. *One battle. One victory!*

95. Germany. (Third Reich). National Socialist Party. *Victory at any price.*

98. China. *From Vol. 4 of the works of Mao Tse-tung: "Learn from comrade Wang-chieh, wholeheartedly for the noble spirit of the Revolution." 1. We are not afraid of suffering; 2. We are not afraid of death.*

99. China. 1968.

100. China. *Improve farm management.*

101. China. *Reap an abundant harvest.* 1968.

102. U.S.S.R. *1917: Glory to the people: 1967.* 1967.

many political parties, despite their ideology, to adopt contemporary art styles is shown especially in posters directed at young voters. Thus, the posters of conservative and labor parties are stylistically often identical. Both parties want to project the image of being in step with the times. Canada's Progressive Conservative Party, as an example, produced a psychedelic art poster done in glow-paint. The caption on the poster reads: "Turn On With The Tories" (Fig. 112).

The style that will be most effective in general is the style that is understandable to the broadest mass of people. Sophisticated art styles often simply do not appeal to the average viewer. Peters urges instead the use of what he calls "objective" art styles. He maintains that the average citizen is not educated to interpret non-objective (or subjective) art, which includes Dadaism, Expressionism, and much other abstraction, as well as Surrealism. If a poster requires too much analysis to be understood, it is useless. Art Nouveau, which is essentially decorative, and certain tendencies in Expressionism can be used. Peters also asserts that for the revolutionary poster (like the war poster), styles that evoke emotion should be chosen.

The art style finally adopted by a political group can tell much about the kind of appeal that it wishes to make. Parties around the world, despite their differences, are using similar modern styles because they are after the same audience — the young voter. With the recent lowering of the voting age from 21 to 18 in the United States, we should be seeing even more contemporary-style posters in election campaigns.

The Socialist Party of Switzerland and the Conservative Party of Finland produced amazingly similar posters for the election year 1968 on the theme of the family man (Figs. 113, 114).

Among the various socialist camps, Cuban poster artists seem to be making an effective appeal to the world's youth with their use of Pop art to convey their messages. The Soviets and the Chinese would appear to have neglected this audience, at least from their failure to make use of modern art styles. Ideological parties in industrialized countries of Europe seem to adopt the most contemporary styles, probably to gain as broad a support as possible.

When a party or pressure group fails to adopt a modern art style, its degree of extremism or moderacy

要使文艺很好地成为整个革命机器的一个组成部分，作为团结人民、教育人民、打击敌人、消灭敌人的有力的武器，帮助人民同心同德地和敌人作斗争

毛泽东

毛主席的革命文艺路线胜利万岁！

103. China. *Hail the defeat of revisionism in our China*. 1967.

104. China. *Agreement on how to love people (soldier), agreement on how to support the army (farmer), firmly responding to Chairman Mao's great wish for "supporting the army and loving the people."* 1967.

106. China. *Long live Chairman Mao.* 1967.

107. Nationalist China. Kuomintang. *Fight for existence by opposing Communism.* 1968.

105. China. *The proletarian revolutionaries rise up and unite under the great red flag of Chairman Mao's thought.* 1967.

108. Nationalist China. Kuomintang. *Fight for freedom by opposing Communism.* 1968.

100. Cuba. *Journey of the heroic guerilla.* 1970.

110. Italy. Republican Party. *Are ideas also not essential? The party with ideas is the party that counts.* 1970.

112. Canada. Progressive Conservative Party. 1968.

111. U.S.A. Committee to Defend the Panther 21. *Power to the People.* 1970.

113. Switzerland. Socialist Party. *For you and your family.* 1968.

114. Finland. Conservative Party. *For the safety of the future.* 1968.

115. Belgium. Socialist Party. *New times, a renewed Belgium. Vote Socialist.* 1968.

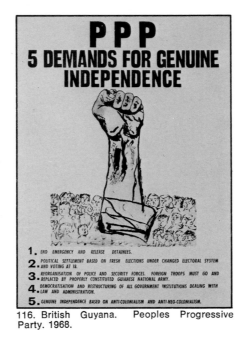

116. British Guyana. Peoples Progressive Party. 1968.

117. Germany (Third Reich). *The people's block: Bavaria.*

can be determined to some extent from its poster design: the Belgium Socialist Party projects a more moderate form of socialism (Fig. 115) than British Guyana's Progressive People's Party (Fig. 116). Further, if one wants to identify the present German political parties that come closest to advocating the principles of National Socialism, it is revealing to compare the style of their poster designs with those used by the Nazis during the Third Reich: there is an uncanny resemblance between the Nazi poster shown in Figure 117 and one of the present day Bavarian Party (Fig. 118). Such graphic comparisons, however, are superficial. Often, parties intentionally try not to communicate their degree of extremism. They wish instead to make the broadest appeal possible and may therefore try to hide extremist tendencies behind the facade of a cool, modern design.

The Use of Symbols and Motifs in Political Graphic Design

A symbol in the political poster is a device for presenting the political message in capsule form. One can write abbreviated political graphic sentences through the incorporation of a number of symbols in a single poster. Symbols frequently suggest meanings directly related to their symbolic form. The dove is a symbol for peace, but the dove as a bird has certain characteristics — gentleness, quietness, and weakness — that lend themselves to the expression of such feelings as love or frailty in the political message. Thus, the famous Czech poster of the dove trapped in a cage (Fig. 119) evokes sympathy from the viewer because of the gentle nature of the animal and the cruel punishment by the captor.

From Pre-Motif to Symbol

To become a symbol in the graphic sense, the element or design must be widely used and recognized. A potential symbol goes through various stages of recognition. First, it is used as a distinguishable element of a picture. This I call "pre-motif." Then, through continued use in a certain area and for a certain period of time, it becomes one of the main elements of the picture. I call this "motif." An example is the factory motif used by the French students to represent the power of the workers (Fig. 120). If the motif becomes universally recognized in a certain area or region, it can be classified as a local or national symbol. If it gains worldwide recognition and use, it becomes an international symbol. An example of a symbol with virtually universal and international recognition is the hammer and sickle.

The clenched fist has, in my opinion, recently graduated from a motif to a symbol. Some examples occur in student posters in France (Fig. 121), Mexico (Fig. 122), and the United States (Figure 123 was labeled the Harvard University fist); in posters of the Black Panthers (Fig. 124); and in posters of women's liberation groups (Fig. 125). The strongest evidence of the development of the fist motif as a symbol is its adoption as the party trademark by France's United Socialist Party (Fig. 126). In fact, this was the same fist design used by the French students.

Labeling Symbols

Certain symbols, through usage, have become identified with left- or right-wing political groups. As an example, fire is a right-wing symbol: witness its use in the torch of the Young Americans For Freedom (Fig. 127) or in the flaming cross symbol of the Ku Klux Klan (Fig. 128). On the other hand, a typical left-wing symbol is the clenched fist.

The left and right usually do not use each other's symbols unless they are using them negatively or in some transformed fashion. An example of how consciously or unconsciously left-wing groups avoid the fire symbol is seen in Figure 129, where the torch of the Statue of Liberty has been removed from the design and replaced by a clenched fist. The symbol has been transformed. What was once a symbol of liberty (torch plus statue) has now become a symbol of women's liberation.

Right-Wing Symbols

The Swastika

The swastika is perhaps the most universally recognized of the right-wing symbols. It was first used as a political symbol in Nazi Germany as the party emblem and the symbol of anti-Semitism. It existed previously as a mystical symbol among various American Indian tribes, and in India, Japan, Persia, and elsewhere. Although many of the political symbols have historical origins, in keeping with the contemporary nature of the book and the collection, I will neglect history and instead show how symbols are used

118. West Germany. Bavarian Party. *Our future: Bavarian Party.* 1969.

119. Czechoslovakia. Students. *Socialism yes, Occupation no!!!* Protesting Soviet invasion. 1968.

120. France. Students. *The fight goes on.* 1968.

121. France. Students. *Down with the deadly cadences* (of the production line). 1968.

122. Mexico. Students. *Not a minute more on our knees.* 1968.

123. U.S.A. "Harvard University fist." 1970.

124. U.S.A. Black Panther Party. Protesting the shooting of the Augusta Six, blacks shot by Georgia policemen. 1970.

125. U.S.A. 1970.

126. France. United Socialist Party (PSU). *A young and revolutionary force lives. Stay with PSU.* 1969.

127. U.S.A. 1969.

128. U.S.A. United Klans of America. 1969.

129. U.S.A. Socialist Workers Party. 1970.

today and then how they can be used effectively in the future. Since new meanings can be associated with old symbols, for practical purposes their history often becomes irrelevant.

The swastika has been adopted by some ultra-right groups of today. Many other right-wing groups, however, hesitate to use this symbol because of its unpleasant associations with the Third Reich. Nevertheless, the National Socialist White People's Party (NSWPP) of Arlington, Virginia, has adopted it to symbolize white power (Fig. 130). Other American Nazi groups also use it.

The Christian Cross

The Christian cross has also become politicized. The cross is used by some Christian democratic parties of Europe, such as the Christian Democrats of Norway (Fig. 131) and the Christian Democrats of Italy (Fig. 132). Although these parties lie close to center on the political spectrum, they profess many of the traditionalist values of their society and, therefore, I classify them on my political spectrum as moderate rightist or conservative. Other users of the cross symbol belong further to the right of the Christian Democrats. These are the Christian Nationalists, such as the Committee for the Reunion of Germany (Fig. 133). Then there are the Christian anti-Communists, such as the Cardinal Mindszenty Foundation (Fig. 134). Even further to the right is the Ku Klux Klan, whose motto, "For God and Country," complements its use of the "fiery cross" as an organizational symbol (Fig. 128).

The Statue of Liberty

The Statue of Liberty as a symbol, although generally used by U.S. groups, has also been used abroad by a Dutch conservative party, the Party For Freedom and Democracy, in the 1968 Parliamentary elections (Fig. 135). This figure has been adopted as the trademark of a number of right-wing groups in the United States. Starting from the far right, it is used by the Liberty Amendment Committee (Fig. 136) and, in fact, by most organizations using the name "liberty." Further left is the American Bar Association Standing Committee on Communism (Fig. 137). The ABA is a pressure group (generally considered conservative). The purpose of the committee is to educate the public about Communism. The ABA's left-wing counter-group is the Lawyers Guild, for which no political symbol

130. U.S.A. National Socialist White People's Party. 1968.

131. Norway. Christian Democratic Party (KDS). *Vote for the new alternative.* 1968.

132. Italy. Christian Democratic Party. *Liberty. Vote Christian Democrats.* 1968.

133. Spain. Committee for the Reunion of Germany. *ACON: Project Oder-Neisse.* Stationery.

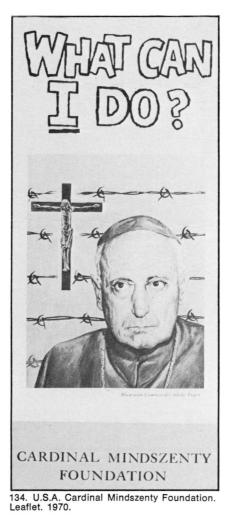

134. U.S.A. Cardinal Mindszenty Foundation. Leaflet. 1970.

135. Netherlands. Conservative Party. *Hold freedom high.* 1968.

136. U.S.A. Liberty Amendment Committee. Leaflet. 1970.

137. U.S.A. ABA Standing Committee on Communism. Leaflet. 1970.

138. U.S.A. American Civil Liberties Union. Magazine advertisement. 1970.

139. France. Union of Youth for Progress (UJP). *Yes to youth. Yes to the region.* 1969.

140. U.S.A. Republican and Conservative parties. James Buckley for Senator Committee (New York State). Bumpersticker. 1970.

has yet been created. An interesting counter-use of the Statue of Liberty symbol was employed by a liberal group, the American Civil Liberties Union, in one of its magazine advertisements (Fig. 138).

The women's liberation use of the Statue of Liberty symbol would seem to refute my theory that it is rightist. But the symbol has undergone a profound transformation (removal of the torch). I doubt that women's liberationists would have adopted it without this modification. The Statue of Liberty, of course, is not only the most identifiable American symbol and unequivocally female, but a massive monument serving as a good power symbol.

The National Flag

The politicization of the national flag has taken place in a number of countries, including France and the United States. The flag is most often used as a political symbol of the right. In France in 1968 the tricolor was used by the Gaullists, generally considered conservative among Frenchmen (Fig. 139). In the United States, the stars and stripes and its colors were used most frequently by the conservative candidates, such as James Buckley, who was elected Senator of New York State (Fig. 140), and George Wallace, running for President (Fig. 13). It has been used all along by such right-wing extremist pressure groups as the Minutemen (Fig 142). It is also used by less-known political groups of the right, such as the Hawaii Foundation for American Freedoms (Fig. 143) and the National Captive Nations Committee (Fig. 144). In the United States today, the Confederate flag enjoys limited use as a political symbol, as in Figure 145 by the Patriot Party, a group of poor southern whites. The latter group, which uses "power to the people" slogans, has adopted the wrong symbol for its cause. The Confederate flag has extreme rightist connotations for many Americans. The Patriot Party is, on the other hand, a leftist group. A mistake in the use of symbols can be detrimental to gaining support. As an example, if the Patriot Party (like other "power to the people" organizations) wishes to attract contributions from wealthy liberals of New York, it might fail. Liberals would identify the Confederate flag with white southern segregation groups, which use it extensively.

The American Eagle

A minor American political symbol also associated with the national flag is the eagle. It has been adopted by the Patriotic Party (Fig. 146) (to be distinguished from the leftist Patriot Party). This symbol is also used by the Christian Crusade (Fig. 147). The eagle, which at present has little international recognition, has great potential, as the dove's counterpart, as an international symbol of war or oppression. The eagle is associated with strength, patriotism, and war. It could be effectively juxtaposed with the dove either by the left or the right. So far this juxtaposition has not been used.

Fire and Lightning

On an international level, fire is used by the Anti-Bolshevik League (Fig. 148). Lightning, a similar symbol of violent light, was used by the Nazis of the Third Reich and became associated with the SS label (Fig. 149). The National White People's Party of the U.S.A. has also adopted it, along with the skull, as a symbol of white power (Fig. 150).

Left-Wing Symbols

The Hammer and Sickle

The hammer and sickle was originally used by the Communists to symbolize the union of workers (the hammer) and peasants (the sickle). The symbol is still used by most Communist parties of the world. In the Soviet Union, it has become so commonplace that it even appears in abstracted form as a design element (Fig. 151). The Soviets, of course, also use the symbol on their national flag. Recently, the Communist parties of industrialized countries seem to be playing down the use of this symbol. Many of the parties of the extreme left have replaced the hammer and sickle with the clenched fist and raised rifle (see below), although there are still some loyal to it, notably the Italian Socialist Party of United Proletarians (Fig. 152).

The Raised Rifle

The raised rifle has become the international motif of armed revolt by liberation groups. It is used by the Cubans (Fig. 153); by the Palestine Liberation groups (Fig. 154); and in the United States by the Black Panthers (Fig. 155) and the Young Lords (Fig. 156).

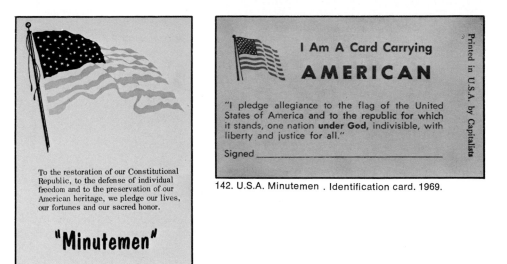

141. U.S.A. Minutemen. Handout. 1969.

142. U.S.A. Minutemen . Identification card. 1969.

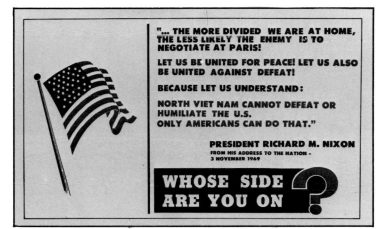

143. U.S.A. Hawaii Foundation for American Freedoms. 1969.

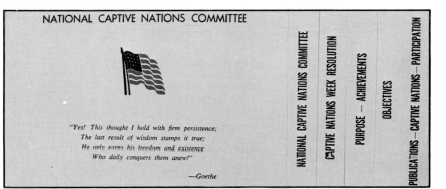

144. U.S.A. National Captive Nations Committee. Leaflet. 1970.

146. U.S.A. Patriotic Party.

145. U.S.A. Patriot Party. 1970.

147. U.S.A. Christian Crusade. Announcement of meeting. 1970.

149. Germany (Third Reich). National Socialist Workers Party (NSDAP). *Waffen SS: Enter at 17. A long or short commitment to serve.*

152. Italy. Socialist Party of United Proletarians (PSIUP). *Against imperialism. For the peace and liberty of the people. For the neutrality of Italy* outside the Atlantic Pact (NATO). *Vote PSIUP.* 1969.

148. Anti-Bolshevik League. Stamps.

150. U.S.A. National White People's Party. 1970.

151. U.S.S.R. *We shall continue in the spirit of the October Revolution and fulfill the five-year plan ahead of time.* 1968.

Peace Symbols

The dove, symbol of peace, is another international symbol of the left. It has been used in numerous ways by the world's peace groups. An interesting variation was produced by the Columbia University Student Mobilization for Peace Committee in New York City, in which the dove's wings were stretched upward like hands in an emphatic plea for peace (Fig. 157). The dove is not only the symbol for the cessation of war, but also, in the United States, it has come to symbolize peace between the races. The juxtaposition of two clasped hands, one black, one white, with the peace dove appropriately illustrates this sentiment (Fig. 158). The dove and the "peace symbol" are frequently combined (Fig. 159).

There is some controversy about the origin and meaning of the emblematic peace symbol, undoubtedly the most important and widely recognized new symbol of the past decade. According to one report, it was invented in 1958 for the Direct Action Committee against Nuclear War; and the design was derived from the letters N and D. The symbol was associated at the outset with the words "unilateral nuclear disarmament." First thoughts on the need for a symbol reflected the obvious practical difficulty of making a large number of long banners bearing these words. The sketch for a symbol was a white circle against a black square, followed by various versions of the Christian cross drawn within the white "sphere." These in turn gave way to the "ND" design.

Lorenz maintains that the symbol has come to be recognized by many Americans as a bomber that has been encircled. The Young Americans For Freedom use a counter-symbol which seems to support Lorenz's "bomber theory" (Fig. 160). In this button, showing a loaded bomber, the derivation can be seen clearly.

Symbols can also become overworked. The peace symbol furnishes a good illustration; it is now being used on almost every conceivable object. The ultimate insult is its appearance on a toilet seat cover (Fig. 161). Political symbols can be so overused that they become meaningless and, eventually, counter-productive.

The well-known symbol for victory, the "V" of World War II, has been turned around (by showing the opposite side of the hand) to mean peace (Fig. 162). But it is also used with its original intent, as seen in the

Mixed Symbols and Motifs

The Hand Motifs

The grasping hand is a typical example of a motif or design element in the pre-symbolic stage. Probably because of its negative connotations, it will remain there. This motif was used by the Dutch Communists in the 1950s (Fig. 164) and by the French students in 1968 (Fig. 165), where it represented the greedy hand of capitalism finally sinking in a sea of revolution. In France the hand appeared again in election campaign posters after the revolt to show how the North Atlantic Treaty Organization and American imperialism had colonized French industry (Fig. 166).

Chain Motifs

The locked chain (Fig. 167) represents for Radio Free Europe the suppression of freedom of thought. The gag over the mouth is used to illustrate suppression of speech (Fig. 168). The breaking chain motif represents the struggle against oppression, and it is used both by the left and the right. This motif has been used by the Soviet Union to represent the African countries' revolt against colonial rule and imperialism (Fig. 169). The Patriot Party breaks chains in a graphic gesture to show the end to oppression of poor whites (Fig. 170). A related motif is the rope motif used by an American right-wing anti-union organization, the National Right To Work Committee (Fig. 171).

Animal Symbols

Animals are favorite political symbols. None, however, have achieved international prominence. They are mainly national or local symbols, such as the panther of the Black Panther Party (Fig. 172) or the two bullocks of India's Congress Party (Fig. 173). The elephant (Fig. 174) is the familiar symbol of the Republican party in America; the donkey is used by the Democrats.

Other Symbols and Motifs

There are many minor symbols and motifs that cannot be easily labeled left or right. Examples are the crossbow motif, used to represent the struggle of the South Vietnamese people

153. Cuba. *1959-1969: Tenth anniversary of the Cuban rebellion.* 1969.

154. Popular Front for the Liberation of Palestine. 1969.

156. U.S.A. Young Lords (American—Puerto Rican liberation group). *I have Puerto Rico in my heart. Young Lords Party.* 1971.

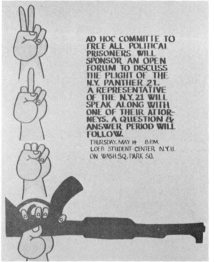

155. U.S.A. Black Panther Party. 1970.

157. U.S.A. Columbia University students, New York City. 1970.

158. U.S.A. Peace poster. Artist: J. Refrebier.

159. U.S.A. Peace poster. Artist: Peter Max. 1970.
160. U.S.A. Young Americans for Freedom. Button. 1970.
161. U.S.A. Toilet seat cover with peace symbol. 1971.
162. U.S.A. New Mobilization Committee to End the War in Vietnam. 1969.
163. U.S.A. National Student Committee for Victory in Vietnam. Bumpersticker. 1969.
164. Netherlands. *If you can't prevent repossession of your property, why not become a subscriber to the* Tribune *(newspaper)?* Newspaper advertisement. 1950.

for independence (Fig. 175). The sun motif (representing rebirth) is used by many Asiatic political groups: in South Korea (Fig. 176), in Japan (Fig. 177), and in Communist China (Fig. 188).

Counter-Use of Symbols

Rightist symbols and motifs appear in many leftist posters as counter-symbols. We have seen this with the Statue of Liberty. The opponent's symbol is used to attract viewers, and the message then destroys the association. A good example is Figure 178: "America, Change it or Lose it." This is a take-off on the now famous slogan of the patriotic right: "America, Love it or Leave it" (Fig. 179). The opponent's symbol can be used to establish negative connotations. This occurs in a Young Americans For Freedom poster, in which the blade of a hammer and sickle symbol is shown piercing the neck of a peace dove (Fig. 195).

The Future of Symbols

Certainly the job of creating new symbols for pressure groups and parties is a difficult one. For large organizations, it may be a matter of hiring a designer to create a new abstract logo. For smaller groups, symbols are generally chosen from everyday objects. In ecology, we may see more plant and wildlife motifs emerge as symbols. Other groups might work with the objects or pictures of the space age as their symbols. The rocket ship, in particular, would seem to have good potential as a symbol in the technological era, since its positive properties include motion, upward direction, power, thrust, and sleekness.

Mode of Presentation

To analyze the various design possibilities, I have adopted the four mode categories established by Janicik in *Art as Propaganda* — portraiture; allegory or metaphor; illustration; "heraldic collocation" — and added a fifth, caricature.

Portraiture may be rendered by photography or illustration. Through continued exposure, the candidate or leader's face and figure come to symbolize the party's cause. Portraiture is the most common type of campaign poster (Fig. 180). In an election campaign, its main purpose is to identify the candidate, but ideological parties also use it in their hero-cult posters.

165.

166.

168.

169.

167.

170.

171.

172.

165. France. Students. *Keep fighting. Capitalism is going under.* 1968.

166. France. Communist Party. *Against the monopolies and their power, who sacrifice the national interest to capitalist profits; uphold the French Communist Party, party of the working class, the people, and the nation.*

167. U.S. Advertising Council of America. 1970

168. Mexico. Students. *Freedom of speech.* 1968.

169. U.S.S.R. *The spark of freedom will not go out.* 1967.

170. U.S.A. Patriot Party. 1970. Announcement.

171. U.S.A. The National Right to Work Committee. 1970.

172. U.S.A. Black Panther Party. 1969.

Mao cult posters produced in Communist China are reported hanging in at least one room of every household (Fig. 181). Cult posters also exist of Lenin (Fig. 182), Castro (Fig. 183), Che Guevara (Fig. 184), Ho Chi Minh (Fig. 185), and Malcolm X, the deceased black leader (Fig. 186).

Allegory and Metaphor. The most popular political allegory represents the good political forces overcoming the evil ones. The Storm, a Palestine liberation group based in Algeria, produced a poster showing a guerilla spearing an octopus with the Star of David emblazoned on it (Fig. 187). The Soviets also use the killing of an octopus to represent the defeat of evil opponents. Figure 189 shows a Greek goddess trampling an octopus with heads of the junta generals who seized power on April 21, 1967. The inscription reads: "People of Hellas, Revolt!"

Schockel wrote that allegory was the ideal mode for the political poster, believing that it stimulates thinking, gives the viewer a vivid impression of any political issue, and can be used to disrobe the opponent of his pretended strength. He adds, however, that it has its drawbacks: "With allegory, it is always difficult to suggest to the onlooker that he is the one represented, especially if something unflattering is said about him. This is because nobody wants to be considered dumb, narrow-minded, conceited, or ugly."

Schockel believes that through the poster one can convince or weaken an opponent. Lorenz, on the other hand, feels that converting opponents should be the last consideration in graphic design. Lorenz asserts that partisans will usually not even bother to look seriously at posters expressing opposing views. I feel that allegory can still be used negatively, if directed at the uncommitted.

Illustration. This is a simple and effective technique and is often used. The slogan "A United Europe" is illustrated by flags interwoven to shape a single flag (Fig. 190). Other posters use photographs or designs to illustrate the promise of happy families (Fig. 191) or more housing (Fig. 192).

Heraldic Collocation. Janicik calls the juxtaposition of symbols with other symbols or in a figure-ground relationship "heraldic collocation." He believes this produces an emblematic effect. Good examples are the coats of arms adopted by nation states. In the seal of the President of the United States, for instance, an eagle is juxtaposed

173. India. Congress Party. *Vote Congress Party of India.*
174. U.S.A. Republican Party. Plastic elephant. 1968.
175. Cuba OSPAAAL. *International week of solidarity with Vietnam.* 1970.
176. South Korea. Democratic Republican Party. *The Democratic Republican Party is the only party that gives the hope of brightening the lives of the people.* 1969.
177. Japan. Liberal Democratic Party. *Is there a country as free as Japan? The party that protects the freedom and does not countenance violence and destruction is the Liberal Democratic Party. Your one vote can improve Japan.*
178. U.S.A. 1970
179. U.S.A. Bumpersticker 1969.

with arrows (war) and an olive branch (peace).

The following are modern examples of heraldic collocation. The juxtaposition of the American flag with the hammer and sickle (Fig. 193) is used to symbolize "the fight by patriotic Americans against Communism." The dove and rifle (Fig. 194) symbolize peace and armed revolt. Juxtaposed, they produce a new meaning. They may be interpreted as "a revolt that will finally bring peace." A Young Americans For Freedom poster (Fig. 195), showing a dove stabbed, is not only an example of the counter-use of symbols, but also of heraldic collocation.

An historical example of heraldic collocation appears in Figure 196, which shows the Christian cross juxtaposed with the swastika in an attempt to produce a positive association. Schockel reports that this poster was designed by the National Socialists for a largely Catholic area of Germany. In order to make Nazism more acceptable to the Catholics, the designer associated the two symbols.

Collocation can be used to convey degrees of intensity of political feelings. As an example, the Communist Party of Israel associates its hammer and sickle with the bulb of a flower to give the impression of moderation (Fig. 197). By contrast, Soviet artists have shown it being held by the strong arms of a steel worker (Fig. 198).

Heraldic collocations allow for the development of a number of new associations. They serve as a shorthand political language. Women's liberation movements in the United States have experimented with it, using the sign for female as their base symbol. This symbol has been juxtaposed with the peace symbol (Fig. 199) and the clenched fist (Fig. 200), the latter containing a third symbol as well — the Statue of Liberty. The torch has been removed and replaced with a clenched fist encircled by the female sign. A women's lib button juxtaposes the equal sign of mathematics with the sign for female (Fig. 201).

Caricature. Poking fun at the opposition through caricature may strengthen the sponsoring party's cause in the mind of the viewer. In the French student revolt of 1968, caricatures were used to mobilize the masses against the Gaullist government by attacking the leader himself. Sometimes De Gaulle was made to look ridiculous

180. Finland. Matti Verkkusen's Coalition. *The country needs a president.* 1968.
181. China. Mao Tse-tung. 1967.
182. U.S.S.R. Lenin. 1968.
183. Cuba. Committee for Defense of the Revolution (CDR).
Let's all go to the plaza with Fidel. 1968.
184. Cuba. OSPAAAL. *Day of the heroic guerilla fighter.*
185. North Vietnam. *My warmest greetings. Determined to win. (Signed) Ho Chi Minh.* Newspaper insert. 1969.
186. U.S.A. Third World Committee. Malcolm X. 1970.
187. Storm (Palestinian commando group). *Storm.* 1969.

支援世界人民的反帝斗争!

188. China. *Support the anti-imperialist struggle of the people of the world.* 1967.

(Fig. 202); at other times he was depicted as a power-hungry dictator (Fig. 203).

The Czech students also used caricature to mock and expose their invaders. Ulbricht, Gomulka, and Brezhnev were made to appear as monsters (Fig. 204). Soldiers were drawn to look like bumbling fools (Fig. 205). The caricatures of Rockefeller during his 1969 visit to South America are similar in intent (Fig. 206).

In the poster "Ford has a redder idea" (Fig. 207), the Ku Klux Klan jabs the opposition with a caricature and a pun. In "Sick of Talk? Want Action!" (Fig. 208), the American Nazi Party tries to expose the "cowardliness" of Negroes in a cartoon showing how to repulse their attacks.

During the Cultural Revolution in Communist China, many caricatures appeared on the walls of buildings identifying some of the leaders as revisionists. In connection with the Vietnam War, the Red Chinese caricatured President Johnson, showing him foolishly putting his head through a noose (Figs. 209, 210).

189. U.S.S.R. *People of Hellas, revolt!* 1969.

190. Italy. Christian Democratic Party (DC). *A United Europe: Vote DC.* 1969.

191. Finland. Liberal Party. The mobilization of liberalism in your best interest. *Choose the Liberal Party.*

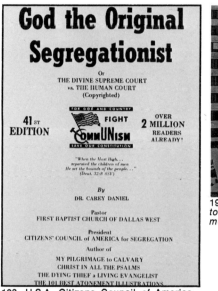

193. U.S.A. Citizens Council of America for Segregation. Leaflet. 1970.

192. Austria. Freedom Party (FPO). *Here, too, buildings should be erected. FPO is more necessary than ever.*

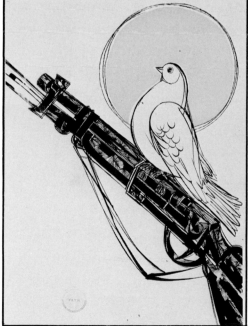

194. Fath. (Palestinian liberation group). 1970.

195. U.S.A. Young Americans for Freedom. 1969.

198.

196.

197.

199.

201.

200.

208.

202.

203.

V PRAZE CHODÍ GODZILA !!
204.

206.

196. Germany (Third Reich) National Socialist Workers Party. *Swastika? Christian cross?*

197. Israel. Communist Party. (Zionist). Announcement of party meeting.

198. U.S.S.R. *Born in the great struggle for the rights of man, the Women's Peasant Alliance remains famous throughout our century.* 1967.

199. U.S.A. Student Mobilization Committee. Button. 1971.

200. U.S.A. Socialist Workers Party. 1970.

201. U.S.A. Women's Lib. Button. 1970.

202. France. Students. *"His master's voice."* Caricature of De Gaulle. 1968.

203. France. Students. *"I am the State,"* Caricature of De Gaulle. 1968.

204. Czechoslovakia. Students. *There's a monster in Prague.* Protesting Soviet occupation. 1968.

205. Czechoslovakia. Students. *"Where is the street, where is the house?"* (Russian folk song). Alluding to the Czech's whitewashing street signs and house numbers to confuse the Soviet invaders. 1968.

206. Latin America. *Wanted: Mr. Nelson Rockefeller, alias "Kerosene."* Inspired by Governor Rockefeller's visit to Latin America. Artist: Juan Sanchez. 1969.

207. U.S.A. United Klans of America. *Ford has a redder idea.* Pun on advertisement slogan, "Ford has a better idea." Leaflet and membership application. 1970.

208. U.S.A. American Nazi Party. Handout. 1967.

209. China. *If the U.S. monopoly capitalist bloc continues to pursue its policy of aggression and war, there will come a day when it will be strangled by the people of the world. The other accomplices of the U.S. will meet the same fate.*

210. China. *All reactionaries are paper tigers. Remember — the style of the reactionaries is fearsome . . . In the long run, the real power does not belong to the reactionaries, but to the people. — Mao Tsetung.* President Johnson's neck in the noose of Vietnam. 1967.

207.

205.

209.

210.

CHAPTER VI

The PLANT Approach

In an age of specialization, political poster design has not escaped efforts to make it a scientific process. The PLANT approach represents such an attempt. This method of public opinion analysis has been applied to U.S. campaigns at both the local and state levels; however, the effectiveness of the technique still remains at issue. The following is a report on the application of the PLANT techniques to political poster design. It was related to me in a series of interviews with its originator, John d'Arc Lorenz. After several sessions, however, Lorenz had not answered all my questions about the technique, insisting that he did not wish to reveal secrets that were very commercially valuable. Therefore, a number of points remain unclarified. I have retained Lorenz's terminology throughout this chapter.

PLANT (Perception/Precinct Level Attitude-Normative Technique) is a survey-research technique applied to all aspects of the election campaign: television commercials, literature, buttons, posters, and even speeches given by the candidate. PLANT has also been used in a limited way for commercial advertising. Lorenz developed PLANT with some associates at the University of Chicago.

PLANT ($P_1 + (C_1 + E_1) -- P_2 + A$ $I=APB$) is a general formula for "scientifically designed" political campaign materials. The formula translates as follows: the initial perception of an individual (P_1), developed by interrelated cultural and environmental factors ($C_1 + E_1$), leads to the perception process an individual manifests prior to solidification of his attitude patterns (P_2). Added to this is his test-determined attitude (A) to social and political issues of the day (I). This all equals attitude-perception-behavior (APB), from which guidelines are drawn that can purportedly be translated into graphic terms.

According to Lorenz, PLANT can be applied specifically to the psychological response of any individual. By understanding this response, one is better able to control or manipulate the poster audience through choice of symbols, words, designs, and colors. The designing of election graphics according to this scientific technique is especially valuable at the local level because one can measure specific audiences.

The use of tested colors and data-extracted symbols can improve the candidate's influence on the electorate in three ways: voters will be able to identify his graphics (recognition); they will associate him with positive ideas (recall); they will be more likely to identify his name in the voting booth (positive identification).

PLANT draws on such fields of research as political science, psychology, anthropology, psychiatry, and color theory. Through the vehicle of a survey-research questionnaire, the potential political poster audience is tested for response to color and symbols, as well as for psychological attitude patterns that may underlie the formation of political opinions. This data is combined with other kinds of research — demographic, sociological, and cultural. PLANT analysts then attempt to convert the data into guidelines for the graphic artist. These include suggestions as to the size of lettering, color combinations, symbols, slogans, and art style.

Color Theory

The color theory of PLANT is said to be more complex than that used in market research. Lorenz maintains that the advertising agencies working for political campaigns are based on the same kind of research that determines which color a housewife prefers for a laundry box. Lorenz wants to determine not only which color, but *why* she prefers it.

He believes that "political" color preferences can be secured for the smallest up to the highest political unit (precinct, district, state, and so forth). Each color is tested for the specific area where the election contest will be held. Lorenz says that one of his tests elicited the following hypothetical color-attitude relationships:

Blue: the color best perceived by moderate conservative-leaning "silent Americans."

Black and white: best perceived by sophisticated urban voters.

Yellow: best perceived by reform-minded voters.

Red: denotes intense feeling, whether from the political right or left.

Orange on blue or red on black: best color combinations for identifying unknown candidates.

Research and Design Phases

The PLANT technique as it applies to the design of election campaign graphics involves six phases.

Phase one: Gathering of what Lorenz calls "hard data." First, all available research on the character of the target audience is collected. Audiences can be divided by regions or class groups. Anthropological studies on such groups as blue-collar workers are readily available in libraries — though these studies must be read very cautiously and critically. Another source of hard data is articles and books by such color theorists as Bernard Levy and Gordon Allport, who have made psychological studies on how individuals perceive colors.

The psychological approach adopted by PLANT generally has its roots in available "hard data." Among the important sources in the field are books by Harold Lasswell, a professor at Yale Law School: *Psychopathology and Politics; Politics: Who Gets What, When and How;* and *World Revolutionary Elites.*

Phase two: Devising of survey-research questionnaire. The PLANT approach provides a link between the "hard data" (existing theoretical works) and the "soft data" derived from the PLANT testing of its target audiences. Since the exact questions asked in the survey are crucial to the success of the technique, they are kept strictly confidential. Lorenz will only reveal that they are unstructured, giving the person interviewed the greatest freedom to express his attitudes on political issues.

There are currently two kinds of surveys being used in political research: the synchronic and the diachronic poll. The synchronic poll involves the measurement of opinions held at the time the poll is taken. Examples are the Gallup and Harris polls. The diachronic poll, which is used in PLANT, measures the psychological attitudes that underlie the opinions surveyed by the public pollsters.

Each survey has at least three parts: attitude statements; true-false answers; and an index of intensity that reveals how much a particular issue excites the individual.

Phase three: Field research. A researcher (usually a political science student) is assigned a specific area. He reads the questions to each respondent and is instructed to write down everything that is said in reply. At the end of the day he submits a written report together with a transcript of all interviews.

Phase four: Content analysis. This is the most important phase of the PLANT technique as it relates to graphic design. The researcher draws from the interviews the key words that reveal the attitudes of the respondent. He carefully tabulates the frequency of such phrases as "American flag," for these are word symbols that can later be converted into graphic symbols. Certain phrases will be converted into slogans for use on posters or in brochures. The word images gathered from these interviews are also used in campaign speeches, television commercials, and brochures produced for the candidate.

Phase five: Formulation of design guidelines. The guidelines may vary in detail and are kept confidential throughout the campaign. They usually include the color combinations to be used. Specific guidelines are also given for the size and positioning of the lettering. The following is an actual sample of instructions for five different brochures and a poster promoting "Candidate X" whose campaign is described later.

Brochures:

#1. Background DARK BLUE with letters in WHITE.

#2. All letters in DARK BLUE on WHITE background.

#3. Print CONFLICT OF INTEREST, CAMPUS DISTURBANCES, etc. as it is in the design of the brochure herein. Print CANDIDATE HAS SOLUTIONS TO STATE'S PROBLEMS in DARK BLUE.
Print the issue statements in DARK BLUE on a WHITE background. DO NOT use the statements through which I have drawn lines.

#4. All material DARK BLUE on WHITE BACKGROUND.

#5. All material DARK BLUE on WHITE BACKGROUND.

Poster:

The background for the poster should be in DARK BLUE. The candidate's picture should be BLUE and WHITE. The letters should be in BRIGHT ORANGE. CAUTION!!!

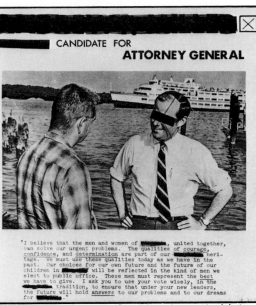

211. U.S.A. Candidate X. (Candidate does not wish to be identified.) 1969

212. U.S.A. Candidate X. (Candidate does not wish to be identified.) 1969.

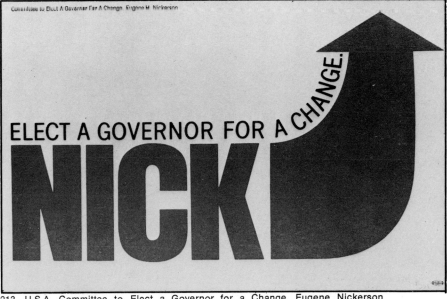

213. U.S.A. Committee to Elect a Governor for a Change. Eugene Nickerson campaigning for Democratic gubernatorial nomination, New York State. 1970

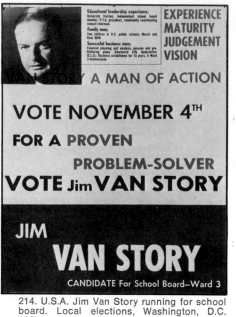

214. U.S.A. Jim Van Story running for school board. Local elections, Washington, D.C. 1969.

PRINT ONLY 5,000 or less of this design.

Phase six: Design of the campaign material. The design process is a team effort involving the art director (of the candidate's advertising agency), the designer, and the PLANT consultant. For a statewide or congressional campaign, the designer may come up with as many as seven or eight design ideas based on PLANT's guidelines. Though this procedure reduces the designer's intuitive processes to a minimum, Lorenz admits that a good graphic designer is still essential to effective political graphics.

The Cost of PLANT

The cost of PLANT for local campaigns can range from $5,000 to $15,-000, depending on the extent of Lorenz's company's involvement in the campaign. These figures include survey research, consulting, and production of graphic guidelines. Lorenz has thus far not billed a candidate separately for his graphic design advice. The actual design work is done by the candidate's advertising agency, with whom Lorenz consults.

Candidate X

Some candidates (Candidate X declined to let us use his name) do not wish to be identified as using the PLANT technique. They fear being accused of manipulating the electorate. The more sophisticated candidates from metropolitan areas are less sensitive about identification with the technique. They see it as a means of pinpointing the needs of the voters, and of projecting their plans and aspirations in the most convincing manner possible.

Lorenz believes that the design used for campaign material must meet the expectations of the voters in that particular area. In a rural southern region, the graphics for Candidate X were decidedly simple, even folksy. For Candidate X's newspaper inserts and brochures, a conventional, almost crude design was chosen, even though the candidate's opponent was using something far more slickly professional. Survey research had apparently revealed that voters in the region associated sophisticated design with out-of-state influence.

In Candidate X's campaign, blue turned out to be the most easily and significantly perceived color for the southern portion of the state. Therefore, blue was used for the brochure to be distributed in that area. Green, on the other hand, tested out best in the northern part of the state. Testing revealed that the candidate's graphics were recognized more often than his opponents' in the northern half of the state, perhaps partially because they were designed in green.

A newspaper insert for Candidate X appeared in the southern and middle sections of the state. The photo used showed Candidate X in shirtsleeves, talking to a working man. Lorenz feels that the identification with working people was successful (Fig. 211). Another newspaper insert, used throughout the state, showed Candidate X standing before his campaign helicopter flashing a victory sign (Fig. 212). The helicopter was supposed to symbolize movement. The colors for this ad were orange and blue with a

215. U.S.A. Republican Party. Sprague for Congress. Peter Sprague running for U.S. congress. 1970.

216. U.S.A. Sprague for Congress. Poster designed by Sprague's nine-year-old son. 1970.

white border. White was used to soften the orange, which, according to Lorenz, is a "high identity color," and must be used in moderate doses. Lorenz indicates that PLANT research shows that too much orange can work against a candidate. The helicopter insert received one of the most positive responses of any piece designed according to the PLANT technique. The candidate won with sixty-four percent of the vote.

The Moot Campaign

The recent campaign of Eugene Nickerson for governor of New York is another instance of the use of PLANT, but it is difficult to evaluate its effect. Lack of funds forced Nickerson out of the race prior to the Democratic primary; his campaign materials, therefore, never got the necessary exposure, and their effect became moot. Research revealed that while Nickerson was well liked he lacked a strong image among voters. The design of a red arrow pointing upward (executed by David Wenman of A C & R Advertising, Inc., a division of Ted Bates) was an attempt to present Nickerson as "forceful," "constructive," and "determined." And the color red was used to intensify this image (Fig. 213).

I interviewed Nickerson to see what he thought about the technique. First of all, he doesn't believe in the importance of graphic materials; he thinks television is more influential. He said, "the poster really doesn't convince anybody in and of itself." Secondly, he was not aware of the unique claims of the PLANT technique, but when I explained the basic premise — influencing attitudes and not opinions — he agreed it was valid.

Nickerson believes that in campaign graphics a good deal of text is needed, with some kind of device to entice the viewer to read it. Although Nickerson never really had a chance to test the PLANT technique, he was satisfied with the work Lorenz had done.

The Non-Victory Victory

Not all PLANT campaigns are victorious. Nevertheless, for Lorenz, even a loss on election day can mean a victory for the technique. When a candidate is faced with formidable odds (anonymity, lack of funds, poor organization), all he can reasonably hope for from PLANT is an increase in his percentage of votes. For example, Jim Van Story was running for a position on the school board in a local election in Washington, D.C. Polls had shown he would get three percent of the vote. He ended up on election day with twelve percent. According to Lorenz, this increase can be attributed to the fact that the PLANT technique was applied not only to his campaign literature but also to his speeches and public statements.

Van Story was running in a predominantly white, upper middle-class area. Testing of the voters in this area elicited the desirability of using bright green or a combination of red on green in campaign posters. The political perception rate for this group was quite high: they were aware of twenty-five percent of the political issues presented to them in the questionnaire (in neighboring states the voters were aware of only four percent of these issues). It was concluded that the symbol focus for this group had to be sophisticated and that the over-all tone of the campaign literature and slogans should be upgraded. These voters were also accustomed to reading more than the average person; hence their eyes moved across a poster in the same way that they read a book (unsophisticated viewers look at a poster as if it were a picture). Lorenz maintains that the "well-read eye" normally focuses five inches from the left hand side of the page, so all pertinent information should begin in this same relative area on the poster. The remaining words on the poster Lorenz considers of secondary importance (Fig. 214).

The Unsatisfied Customer

Peter Sprague, the Republican candidate (1970) for Congress from New York's 15th District, did not like the PLANT poster designed for his campaign (Fig. 215). It annoyed him so much that he fired the agency that designed it. Sprague reported that he received many complaints about the poster: that it didn't have a political message and that it was frivolous. He also maintains that the poster had technical flaws; for instance, the type was too small — it could not be read from a moving bus.

Sprague substituted instead a poster designed by his nine-year-old son (Fig. 216.) The boy chose a flower motif because "flowers are life and life begins things." It is doubtful that this poster is any less frivolous than the original, but the youth of its creator managed to generate interest and even television coverage.

Sprague gained the best publicity of his campaign, but he lost the election.

Lorenz defends Sprague's poster as specifically designed to identify a totally unknown candidate to the electorate. The blue and white color combination was also tested as having the highest recognition level for the residents of New York City, where the election took place. Other posters had been planned for Sprague, but because of the high cost of producing them and the shortage of campaign funds, they could not be produced.

* * *

Lorenz agrees that graphic design alone cannot win an election campaign. Intelligent use must be made of other media. However, for the candidate with limited funds, or for the local candidate who cannot generate publicity on radio and television, the poster is of considerable importance. Effective design becomes more crucial to his chances of victory. Even the candidate who can afford the high-priced media should not eliminate printed material from his campaign.

One of the drawbacks of the PLANT approach, as the reader is no doubt aware, is that there is no scientific method of measuring its effects. Voting returns provide a clue, but they are difficult to analyze in evaluating the success of one particular propaganda technique. Nevertheless, Lorenz states that the effect of the technique can be gauged to some extent *during* the campaign by noting such things as whether voters are beginning to wear PLANT buttons more than the buttons of other candidates. Also, PLANT has begun conducting surveys after the graphics have been distributed (but before the actual election) to try to determine their impact. No results are available, however.

If PLANT or a variation of this approach is the direction in which political graphic design is headed, what does this mean for the voter? Will he become an unknowing victim of manipulative techniques? Lorenz answers: "The voter's mind is too complex to be totally manipulated by a color or a symbol," adding that "the individual is a fragile unit, composed of complex socialized attitudes reflecting the political culture of his society. Symbols, words, and colors are vehicles by which message-fragments of the political culture itself can be communicated. Better designed and researched posters and other campaign materials are simply better communications vehicles."

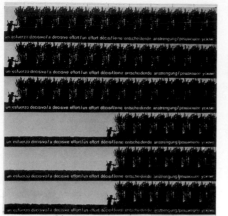

217. Cuba. Committee for the Defense of Revolution (CDR). 1970.

218. Cuba. Billboard with picture of Castro. 1970.

219. Cuba. OSPAAAL. *Day of solidarity with Guatemala.* 1970.

CHAPTER VII

Production and Distribution

The French Student Experience

In his book *Kunst und Revolte,* Peters describes the team effort employed by the students of the Beaux-Arts in Paris during the May-June uprising of 1968. On Monday, May 13, 1968, one million students and workers of Paris staged a general strike in the Latin Quarter. Students occupied the university buildings and settled in for an extended strike. The art students of the Beaux-Arts occupied their own building and formed various design and production committees.

The Atelier Biarchon was renamed the Atelier d'Affiches Populaires ("People's Poster Studio") and became the poster production center of the strike.

The students first printed leaflets and handouts that explained their position to the people. Later, they began to turn out pictorial posters, of which an estimated 120,000 were produced during the strike. There were, in all, over 300 different posters, in average editions of between two and three hundred each. Other art student groups, also producing their own posters, formed simultaneously in Nantes, Marseilles, Montpelier, and Dijon.

Production Rooms

The production of posters involved a highly organized and controlled system. The Atelier consisted of six rooms, one for design, one for production (the making of the screens), and four for the actual printing (lithography and serigraphy). In all, two hundred students took part in the production of posters; at any one time there were between thirty and eighty students working. Production continued around the clock. Classrooms were converted into sleeping quarters, and many students never left the building. Orders for posters came in from all areas around Paris. These included requests by union groups, such as taxi drivers, and factory committees.

The Blackboard

In the design room stood a large blackboard upon which final texts of slogans were written. These had been approved by a special committee. The artists selected their basic materials from the slogans on the board. They then submitted sketches to an assembly of the students elected to choose the best designs. The artist was kept under constant supervision and was frequently asked to improve or omit something. Criteria for designs were "readability" and effectiveness; thus many sketches were rejected. Peters says that here not only was the process of art evaluation democratized, but so was its production.

Control Points

The Atelier established a number of control points around its headquarters that were meant to keep out the police and strangers. Students were briefly interrogated at the check points to determine whether they were loyal to the cause.

The student and worker representatives from sections of Paris came to these control points to pick up their posters. There they were required to show identification. Before any of the posters were allowed to leave the Atelier, they were stamped and assigned to a certain section of Paris for posting. This, according to the students, prevented the posters from ending up in the suitcases of Americans as collector's items.

The shortage of money to buy paper and paint finally brought the art students' work to a standstill, but the phrase coined by the French students, "La lutte continue" ("The fight goes on") (Fig. 120), was reflected in the poster production of students around the world. The same methods were used in Czechoslovakia (August, 1968), in Mexico (Summer, 1968), and in New York City (Spring, 1970). At New York University alone, the Art Students Peace Committee was reported to have produced 40,000 posters. The propaganda methods of the Atelier Populaire have also been duplicated in Asia and South America.

Hundreds of pressure groups around the world are now producing posters with homemade silkscreen presses. The low cost of the process makes it accessible to small, poor political groups. Consider the great disparity between the cost of a few thousand sheets of paper, paints, a wooden frame, a silkscreen (under $100) and the large expense of one television or radio spot (from as much as $1,000 up). If posters are well distributed throughout a city, they may even have greater impact than radio or television. Poster production and distribution for large political parties is more complex. For these groups, printings run into the millions of copies, and nationwide distribution channels are needed. The rental of advertising space is also necessary. As an example of the comparative differences in cost between posters and television in New York City, the following tables are revealing. New York Transit Advertising charges for poster display in the subways are:

City-wide rate for 30″ x 45″ (one sheet) poster:
Minimum coverage (300 posters)
$3,190 per month
Representative coverage
(600 posters) $6,110 per month
Estimated exposure:
218 million exposures per month (based on 109 million fares per month multiplied by two, which assumes one exposure at entrance and one at exit). Four and one-half million people ride the subway daily.

Comparable rates for television (WNBC-TV Rate Card #38, effective September 14, 1970 — 50% discount for political advertising New York City area):
Prime Time (6:59 p.m. - 11:59 p.m.)
10 seconds $450
Estimated exposure:
620,000 homes (1.5 - 2 people per home).

It thus seems possible that even for the well-financed, large political organization, the poster may be the most effective and cheapest way to reach the largest audience. The question of impact of the two types of message remains debatable.

Election Campaigns

Large political parties also design their posters in the manner of a team effort, although not as informally as the French Atelier. The political party team usually consists of the art director, the campaign manager, the designer, and the candidate.

220. Cuba. OSPAAAL. *Day of solidarity with the Afro-American people.* 1970.

221. Cuba. OSPAAAL. *Day of solidarity with the people of Venezuela.* 1970.

222. China. Advertisement for Guozi Shudian. 1970.

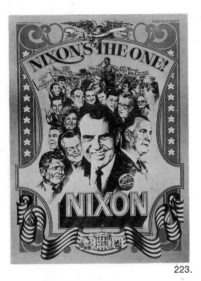

223.

224.

225.

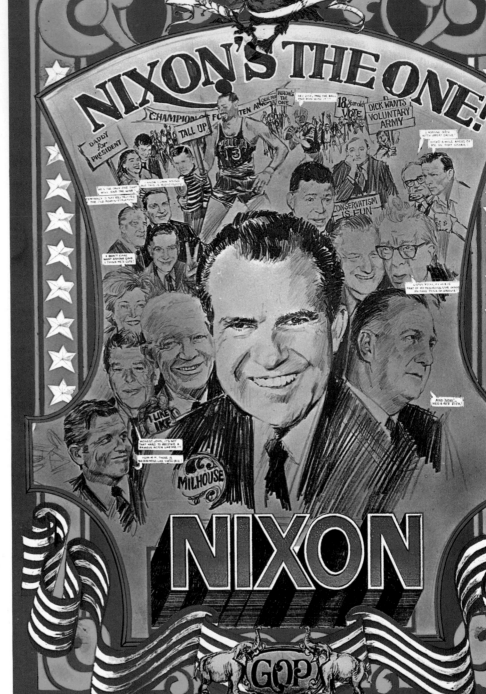

223-226. U.S.A. Republican Party. Youth for Nixon Committee. The four designs on this page are preliminary sketches for poster to elect Nixon. Final published poster can be seen on page 94. (Figure 307). 1968.

Resolutely Support the Anti-imperialist Struggles of the People of Asia, Africa and Latin America.
Soutenir fermement la lutte anti-impérialiste des peuples d'Asie, d'Afrique et d'Amérique latine
Firme apoyo a la lucha antiimperialista de los pueblos de Asia, Africa y América Latina

227. China. *U.S. Imperialism must get out of all places it occupies.* 1967.

228. China. *Oppose racial discrimination.* 1967.

229. U.S.S.R.
Get out of Arab territory! (directed at Israel). 1968.

230. Fatah (Palestine liberation movement). 1969.

The "Nixon's the One" poster (Fig.226) was produced by the Youth for Nixon Committee during the 1968 U.S. Presidential election campaign. Figures 223, 224, and 225 show the intermediary design stages. In the final version, notice the arrangement of the heads of the various Republican leaders: Nixon is the largest, Agnew comes second, Lindsay (before his switch to the Democratic Party) and Rockefeller run a close third, and Reagan is not far

behind in fourth place. The emphasis here is on party unity. The careful positioning of the heads visually harmonizes various strains of Republicanism — Hatfield (flashing a peace sign), a liberal, and Goldwater, a conservative, are in the same poster. In the background are the cultural heroes (including a movie actress, a cowboy, and a sports star who is also black — Wilt Chamberlain). Further back are people cheering and demonstrating for Nixon. The poster has youth appeal because it combines the traditional American campaign election poster style with some contemporary paraphernalia, such as the button with the catchy word "Milhous." The poster was sold on college campuses for fifty cents in order to raise money for the presidential campaign.

The World's Largest Poster Producers and Distributors

As a group, local political parties produce and distribute the largest volume of posters during election campaigns. But poster production by propaganda agencies occurs on a more continuous basis and has a greater impact internationally. The largest agencies are located in Cuba, China, and the Soviet Union. Palestine liberation groups dispersed throughout the Arab countries produce political posters for export. All of them,

with the exception of the Soviet Union, produce multi-language posters. The most common languages are English, Spanish, and French, and, because of the Palestinian conflict, Arabic. The multi-language poster is truly an international political medium.

Poster distribution channels are very similar. One centralized agency sends posters by mail to local bookstores or diplomatic consulates, where they are donated or sold to the public. In addition, mailing lists are kept of individuals who receive posters and other propaganda literature regularly at their homes.

Cuban Agencies

Cuba has both an internal and international poster producing agency. The former is called CDR (Committee for the Defense of the Revolution) and the latter OSPAAAL (Organization for Solidarity Among the People of Asia, Africa, and Latin America).

CDR is the ideological arm of the Cuban Communist Party. In the traditional Communist manner, its posters are often designed to encourage workers to increase productivity (Fig. 217). CDR also sponsors billboards to inspire work and revolutionary zeal throughout Cuba's countryside (Fig. 218).

OSPAAAL's primary purpose is to coordinate activities and act as a communications center for its Third World members. OSPAAAL supplies guerilla movements with propaganda and financial aid. It has spread news and propaganda about nearly every significant revolutionary activity in the Third World, and in many cases has promoted small nationalist movements into international ones.

The publishing arm of OSPAAAL, located in Havana, is the most prolific poster-producing agency in any socialist country. OSPAAAL posters are sent by mail to individuals, student groups, and socialist organizations around the world. They are also distributed by Cuban embassies and consulates, including the Cuban mission to the United Nations in New York City. The posters have a common theme, "solidarity with oppressed peoples." Some examples are "solidarity with" Guatemalan (Fig. 219), Afro-American (Fig. 220), and Venezuelan (Fig. 221) peoples.

China's Four-Languages Press

Four Languages Press (Guozi Shudian), located in Peking, is another large international distributor of posters, servicing franchised bookstores

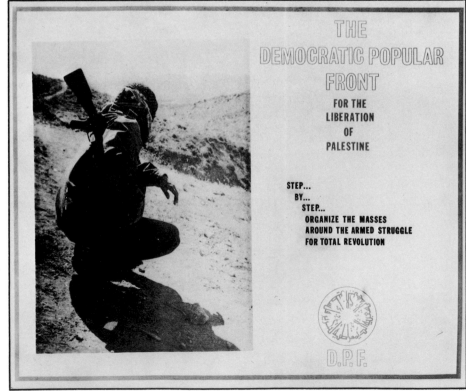

231. Democratic Popular Front for the Liberation of Palestine. 1969.

throughout the world (Fig. 222). In the United States there are two such stores; one in New York and one in San Francisco. The posters are produced in what the Chinese refer to as the four colonial languages (English, Spanish, French, and Arabic).

The poster themes are of a local (internal politics) and international character. Popular subjects are U.S. imperialism (Fig. 227) and black liberation (Fig. 228).

Production in the Soviet Union

In the Soviet Union, Soviet Artist's Publishers solicits various artists' collectives, such as the Kalinsky Poligraph Kombinat located in the city of Kalinin, for poster designs and publishes them for distribution throughout the country. These posters are also sent abroad through Mejdu Narodnia Knigi (International Book Distributors) to Soviet embassies and Russian bookstores. Some poster themes are international. They include criticism of American involvement in Vietnam, calls for revolution against all "fascist regimes," and particularly threats to Israel to get out of Arab territory (Fig. 229). Large poster editions (25,000 to 500,000) are proof of the importance the Russians attach to this form of propaganda.

Soviet posters have not appeared in other than Russian language editions. But because of their heavy pictorial content they can be easily understood by an international audience. Soviet embassies stock them as gifts for their visitors. Some bookstores in Europe and the United States (usually Russian bookstores) also sell them. In addition, large quantities are brought back by tourists visiting the Soviet Union. The Dom Knigi, a three story bookstore in Leningrad, is always well-stocked with at least fifty different poster designs.

Palestinian Liberation Organizations

There are a number of Palestinian liberation organizations producing and distributing posters. The printing is largely done in Lebanon, Algeria, Egypt, and Jordan by such groups as Fatah (Fig. 230) and the Democratic Popular Front for the Liberation of Palestine (Fig. 231). In the United States, these posters are distributed by sympathetic student organizations, and such socialist groups as the Young Socialist Alliance both reprint and distribute them (Fig. 232). Many of the Palestinian posters are in English or French. The Palestinian groups use Arabic in their posters and poster

232. U.S.A. Young Socialist Alliance. 1970.

233. U.S.A. Advertising Council of America. 1971.

stamps which are designed specifically to raise money for weapons and to recruit guerilla fighters.

American Propaganda

Although the United States has an international propaganda agency, United States Information Agency (USIA), it does not use posters. USIA instead "exports culture," mainly in the form of American books and art and industrial exhibitions.

Internally, the government has no centralized propaganda agency. Each department does its own poster advertising. Many of these public service programs are carried out in conjunction with the Advertising Council of America. Some of the poster themes are U.S. savings bonds (Fig. 233), the hiring of war veterans (Fig. 234), and recruitment for the various armed forces.

234. U.S.A. Advertising Council of America. 1971.

235. U.S.S.R. "Baby Lenin" pin. 1967.

CHAPTER VIII
Poster Substitutes

THIS AD INSULTS WOMEN

THIS AD INSULTS WOMEN

236. U.S.A. Women's Liberation. Sticker. 1970.

A UNIVERSE CALENDAR

the liberated woman's appointment calendar and survival handbook 1971

237. U.S.A. Appointment. 1971.

Poster substitutes serve the same function as posters, whether their size is as small as a postage stamp or as large as a billboard, or their shape is as awkward to print on as a ballpoint pen. Each propaganda art object serves as a miniature Trojan horse upon which the propagandist can transport his message. His audience may put it on his person, bring it into his home, or pass it on to his family and friends. Some of the objects on which a propaganda message has typically been placed are: ashtrays, pencils, banners, brochures, bumperstickers, business cards, buttons, calendars, coasters, dresses, drinking glasses, envelopes, flags, greeting cards, hats, kerchiefs, key chains, kites, matchbook covers, neckties, pins, postcards, plastic wraps, record jackets, stamps, soft-drink cans, stickers, stationery, statuettes, tattoos, T-shirts, and wrist watches.

The appearance of poster substitutes does not necessarily imply a diminishing use of posters. Substitutes can be considered as an additional tool in reaching the public, in surrounding voters with a candidate's presence — in short of creating a saturation effect. The theory of saturation is as follows: if the candidate is *everywhere*, he must be running strong (and have money and efficiency behind him). For party propagandists, the motivation is the same: all media reinforce consciousness of the party's principles and, indeed, an awareness of the existence of the party itself.

Buttons and Bumperstickers

Next to posters, buttons and bumperstickers are probably the most ubiquitous campaign materials in the United States. These substitutes are more personal than the poster: when someone chooses to wear a button or place a bumpersticker on his car, he personally and publicly endorses a political cause. Their use implies a voluntary commitment; if an individual sees a large crop of buttons, he may be convinced that the candidate or leader is very popular. For members of ideological parties and supporters of underdog candidates, the public espousal of the cause is an expression of strength — it takes courage to hold a minority viewpoint — and helps give a feeling of solidarity.

The bumpersticker is a peculiarly American phenomenon.

Ideological propagandists believe strongly in the long-term effectiveness of personalized cult objects to reinforce party doctrines. The Soviet Communists, as an example, sell many personal items with Lenin's name imprinted on them. The height of propaganda cultism is the "baby Lenin pin" (Fig. 235). This pin is a miniature photograph of Lenin as a baby, framed in a red plastic star. Some Soviets wear it religiously on their lapels; others, especially students, mock its use as a reflection of the excesses of personality cultism. Lenin's image also graces the covers of children's books and students' notebooks. Stationery and billboards bear his image.

The Sticker as a Sabotage Device

The sticker, despite its small size, can have a major impact on an audience, because it can be affixed to almost any surface quickly and easily. It is particularly effective in subverting a poster message. For instance, the "This ad insults women" sticker (Fig. 236) was designed by a women's lib group to be stuck on commercial advertising posters that portray women as sex objects. Stickers with a deprecating message can be put on a candidate's posters and other campaign material, with an enormously disrupting effect.

"Trojan Horses"

Many poster substitutes are designed as practical items that can be presented as gifts. Along with the gift, of course, goes the political message. Much can be said for this indirect approach. The calendar, as an example, is an effective propaganda piece because it is more likely to be taken into the home and used on a daily basis than the poster. A further refinement of the calendar is the appointment book (Fig. 237). Greeting cards with political

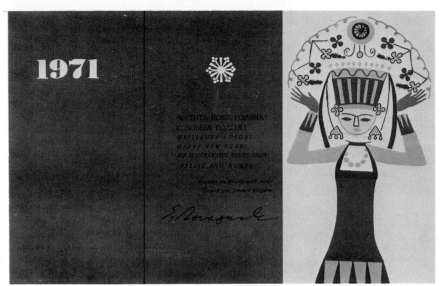

238. Bulgaria. The Committee for Bulgarian Women. Happy New Year Card. 1971.

messages provide another opportunity to propagandize (Fig. 238). The propaganda postage stamp (a miniature poster), although it has no mail service value, can be placed on envelopes, like Christmas seals, as a sign of support for the cause. Such groups as the Anti-Bolshevik League (Fig. 239) sell their stamps to raise money for the organization.

In the United States, many political candidates have recently given away poster substitutes that have practical use, such as a lady's rain bonnet or shopping bag, printed with the name of the candidate or a party slogan. The person wearing or carrying the object both advertises the cause and makes a gesture of personal support.

Some campaign consultants, among them National Democratic Party chairman Larry O'Brien, who managed John F. Kennedy's successful campaign, maintain that poster substitutes are a waste of campaign funds. I feel, however, that most election candidates would not agree. Substitutes often serve as "security blankets" for these candidates, making them feel that they have done everything possible to increase their chances for victory. In addition, the saturation effect produced by substitutes can, in many cases, aid in identifying the candidate and showing the strength of his popular support.

239. Anti-Bolshevik League. Stamps. 1970.

CHAPTER IX

The Law and Prop Art

Historically, political posters have been subject to some form of government censorship. On July 28, 1971, the French government issued a law stating that only official posters could be printed with black letters on white paper. In 1818, a law was passed requiring each French poster to have a tax stamp, regardless of its color. In Russia, during the time of the Revolution, inscriptions appeared on the bottom of protest posters warning that removal of the poster would be a "counter-revolutionary act."

In pre-World War I Germany, the police censored posters criticizing the government. Later, the Prussian Press Act, Article 9, forbade all political posters with the exception of announcements for legally approved meetings, public entertainment, and commercial advertising.

Poster Display and Free Speech

In the United States, the public display of controversial posters and even poster substitutes is related to a central constitutional issue: whether freedom of speech can be limited for any reason. The display of political posters is a form of expression protected by the First Amendment. But free speech and poster display may be limited when there is a "clear and present danger" to the public safety.

The following cases generally uphold the right to political display, while recognizing the limiting doctrine.

People v. *Yolen* was a case in New York City Criminal Court in 1966 that involved a regulation of the Parks Department prohibiting the flying of kites in parks for advertising or political purposes. The regulation read: "No person shall distribute, display, transport, carry or construct any flag, banner, sign, emblem, model device, pictorial representation, or other matter within any park or park-street for ad-

vertisement or political purposes. Nor for the same purposes shall any person display by means of aircraft, kite, balloon, aerial bomb or any other device, any flag, banner, sign or any other matter above the surface of any park or park street" (Article II, Section 6). The defendant, Yolen, flew a kite in Central Park advocating the election of John V. Lindsay as mayor. The court found the regulation an unconstitutional abridgement of the First Amendment guarantees. The prosecution had clearly failed to establish any clear and substantial connection between the regulation prohibiting political kites and the possible danger to the safety, comfort and convenience of the people of the city in their use of the public parks.

Two decisions relating to the distribution of "freedom buttons" were handed down in 1966 by the Court of Appeals of the Fifth Circuit. The first, *Burnside* v. *Boyers,* involved a high-school regulation prohibiting students from wearing buttons that had the words "One Man One Vote" and "SNCC" printed on them. (The buttons had been produced by the Student Nonviolent Coordinating Committee.) The school regulation that forbade the wearing of buttons on school property was declared unconstitutional under the First and Fourteenth Amendments. The court held that only if the decorum of the classroom had been disturbed by the presence of "freedom buttons" would the school principal have been acting within his authority.

Blackwell v. *Issaquena County Board of Education* was a case in which the court felt that the banning of buttons was justified. The facts of this case are memorable. One day thirty pupils wore "freedom buttons" to class, and they were told by the prinicipal not to bring them back again. The next day, however, even more students showed up wearing the buttons and began distributing them to their classmates in the school building. Distribution activities became so exuberant that the students pinned buttons even on those who didn't want to wear them. One student made a younger child cry by pinning a button on him. Charles Cole, a bus driver, entered the school building with a cardboard box full of buttons and began distributing them. Cole went into the classrooms without · permission, handing out buttons. Other students threw buttons into the school building through the windows. In this case, the court held that the regulation of school

authorities prohibiting students from wearing such buttons was reasonable. It concluded that the distribution of buttons led to a complete breakdown of school discipline. The button that created all this commotion depicted a black and a white hand joined together and the letters "SNCC."

Display on Public Transportation Vehicles

During the last three years, with a rise in the use of graphics by anti-war protest groups, the issue of whether public transit companies should be allowed to ban their advertising has become of major importance. Although most anti-war posters are pasted illegally on the walls of buildings or subway platforms, the question is whether the dissenters have the right to place paid advertisements in the manner of the established political parties. The issue was resolved by the courts in California and New York.

The first and most important case took place in a federal court *(Kissinger* v. *New York City Transit Authority).* Members of the Students for a Democratic Society sought a declaratory judgment that the N.Y.C. Transit Authority be required to rent space to them. They wished to display on the walls of subway station platforms two posters of a child with a scarred back and arm, with the following inscription: "Why Are We Burning? Torturing? Killing? The People of Vietnam?"

The Transit Authority refused to display the posters. It contended that it limits the advertising it will accept to (a) commercial advertising for the sale of goods, etc.; (b) public service announcements; and (c) political advertising at the time of and in connection with elections. The Transit Authority also contended that the posters were provocative and inflammatory and would be displayed to a large "captive audience" in the confined area of the subway. Under these circumstances, they asserted that the posters would likely cause serious disturbances, disorder, and vandalism, endangering safety in the subways and interfering with the transportation of passengers. The court held that there was not sufficient evidence to show that the posters would present a "clear and present danger" to the public safety, and therefore the guarantee of freedom of speech under the First and Fourteenth Amendments was extended to the anti-war posters.

Two other cases, the *Hillside Community Church* case and the *Wirta Alameda-Contra Costa Transit* case, both upheld the right of peace groups to advertise on public transportation vehicles in California.

In the *Hillside* case, anti-war posters sponsored by the Peace Committee of the Hillside Community Church were refused display by the Tacoma Transit Company. The court held that although the city of Tacoma was acting in a proprietary capacity when accepting advertising, political posters were still within the orbit of constitutional guarantees. The *Wirta* case involved a Women's Strike for Peace poster, with the legend " 'Mankind must put an end to war or war will put an end to mankind' — John F. Kennedy." The court ruled that even though the poster was a "paid advertisement" it must not be denied the protection of the First Amendment.

None of the above information should be taken as final advice for the poster distributor. Since the law is continually changing, it is best to contact a lawyer for any questions regarding the legal status of specific posters.

The Poster Gallery

SECTION I.

Election Campaigns, 1967 to 1971

This section covers election posters in their widest sense: not only the direct appeals for votes but also for many of the events and processes in a campaign, such as party nominations, announcements and meetings.

Election Candidates

Although elections produce the largest volume of posters, it will quickly be evident from the samples in this section that they are not among the most interesting ones graphically. This section has been divided into election posters which focus on the candidate and those which highlight the work of the party.

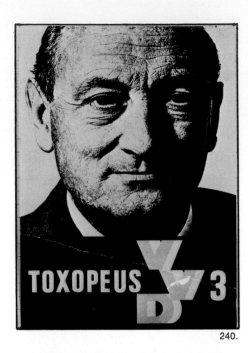

240.

244.

CANDIDATE IDENTIFICATION

240. Netherlands. People's Party for Freedom and Democracy (VVD). 1968.

241. France. Democratic Union of the Republic (UDR). *Pompidou: He sticks to his promises.* Presidential elections, 1969.

242. Denmark. Center Party.

243. Norway. Liberal Party. *Now it will happen. Vote row D.* 1969.

244. West Germany. Christian Socialist Union (CSU).

245. U.S.A. Republican Party. New York State. Committee to Keep Senator Goodell Senator Goodell. Charles Goodell running for U.S. Senate. 1970.

246. U.S.A. Democratic Party. New York State. Committee to Make Ottinger Senator Ottinger. Richard Ottinger running for the U.S. Senate. 1970.

247. Great Britain. Conservative Party. Candidate Heath (present prime minister). 1970.

248. Austria. Freedom Party (FPO). *Gotz for Graz.* 1967.

249. U.S.A. Democratic Party. Edmund Muskie running for Vice President. 1968.

250. Australia. Labor Party. 1968.

251. U.S.A. Democratic and Liberal Parties. New York State. Committee to Re-elect Ryan to Congress. William F. Ryan running for U.S. Congress. 1970.

248.

POMPIDOU

il tient
ce qu'il promet

241.

CENTERN

242.

Nu skal det ske
☓D VENSTRE

243.

Keep Senator Goodell
Senator Goodell.

He wrote the first legislation to end the war. 44 major pieces of legislation in 22 months.

He's too good to lose.

245

Ottinger
for Senator

Committee to Make Ottinger Senator Ottinger

246.

ACTION
not
words

VOTE
Conservative

247.

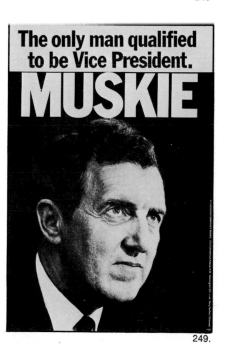

The only man qualified
to be Vice President.
MUSKIE

249.

join the swing to
GOUGH WHITLAM
and Australian Labor

250.

RE-ELECT WILLIAM F. RYAN
Democrat-Liberal

NEW YORK'S CONGRESSMAN FIGHTING
FOR PEACE·HUMAN RIGHTS·CITIES

251.

252.

253.

254.

255.

256.

252. Sweden. People's Party. *Your vote for the People's Party will get results.* 1968.

253. Ireland. Fine Gael. 1970.

254. U.S.A. Democratic Party. New York State. Arthur Goldberg running for governor. 1970.

255. Australia. Labor Party. 1968.

256. Australia. Labor Party. 1968.

257. Finland. Electoral Committee for Urho Kekkonen. *Statesman, President.*

258. France. Centrist Party. *Alain Poher: A President for all the French.* 1970.

259. U.S.A. Republican Party. California. Ronald Reagan running for governor.

260. Chile. Christian Democratic Party. *Hold tight. Alessandri will return.* 1970.

261. Chile Christian Democratic Party. *Alessandri will victoriously return.* Presidential elections. 1970.

262. Chile. Christian Democratic Party. Presidential elections, 1970.

VALTIOMIES
PRESIDENTTI

URHO KEKKOSEN VAALILIITTO

257.

ALAIN POHER
UN PRÉSIDENT
POUR TOUS
LES FRANÇAIS

258.

A PROVEN WINNER
GOV. REAGAN

259.

¡AGUÁNTENSE!
¡ALESSANDRI
VOLVERÁ!

1970

260.

2
Victorioso
Volverá

ALESSANDRI

261.

ALESSANDRI

262.

263.

264.

265.

266.

267.

268.

269.

270.

271.

Damit Sie
auch morgen
in Frieden
leben
können.

SPD

272.

263. New Zealand. Labour Party.

264. Canada. New Democratic Party. 1968.

265. France. Federation of Left Democrats and Socialists. *François Mitterand asks you to vote for Annie Duperrey.* Legislative elections. 1967.

266. Chile. Christian Democratic Party. *Popular triumph! Tomic.* 1970.

267. Canada. Social Credit Party. *Man of the people. Vote Réal Caouette.* 1968.

268. Great Britain. Cooperative Party. 1970.

269. West Germany. Social Democratic Party (SPD).

270. Ireland. Fine Gael. Presidential elections, 1970.

271. West Germany. Social Democratic Party (SPD) *Guaranteed employment and a stable economy.* Karl Schiller running for Economics Minister. 1970.

272. West Germany. Social Democratic Party (SPD). *So that tomorrow to you can live in peace.* Willy Brandt running for Chancellor. 1969.

273.

274.

275.

276.

FOR
AMERICA
VOTE

MADDOX

277.

279.

A better city for everyone.

PROCACCINO
lawyer, educator, judge, comptroller

280.

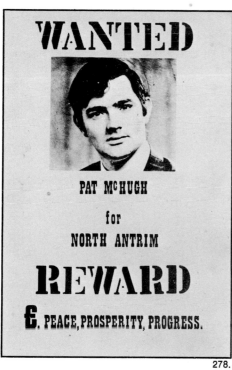

WANTED

PAT MᶜHUGH

for

NORTH ANTRIM

REWARD

£, PEACE, PROSPERITY, PROGRESS.

278.

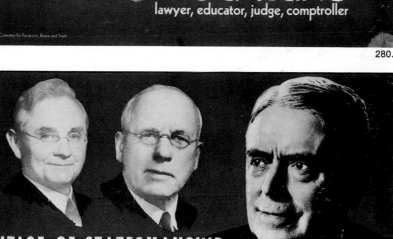

HERITAGE OF STATESMANSHIP...

VOTE... AND VOTE LABOUR AGAIN

281.

CANDIDATE
IDENTIFICATION
CONTINUED

273. India. Congress Party. *The unity, prosperity, and progress of the country is with the Congress Party. Vote Congress.* Indira Gandhi.

274. Great Britain. Conservative Party. Edward Heath running for Prime Minister. 1968.

275. France. Union of the Democratic Republic (UDR). *Yes, DeGaulle wants progress. With you, for you.* 1967.

276. U.S.A. Republican Party. Richard M. Nixon running for President. 1968.

277. U.S.A. Democratic Party. Georgia. Lester Maddox running for governor.

278. Northern Ireland. Labour Party. 1969.

279. U.S.A. Liberal Party. N.Y.C. John Lindsay running for mayor. 1969.

280. U.S.A. Democratic Party. New York City. Independent Citizens' Committee for Procaccino, Beame and Smith. Mario Procaccino running for mayor. 1969.

281. New Zealand. Labour Party.

282.

283.

287.

CANDIDATE IDENTIFICATION
CONTINUED

282. U.S.A. Democratic Party. Kennedy for President. Robert F. Kennedy campaigning for Democratic Presidential nomination. 1968.

283. Great Britain. Conservative Party. Edward Heath promises to bring Britain into the Common Market. 1970.

284. U.S.A. Republican Party. Pennsylvania. George Goodling running for U.S. Congress. 1970.

285. U.S.A. Democratic Party. Wisconsin. Citizens for Proxmire Committee. William Proxmire running for U.S. Senate. 1970.

286. U.S.A. Peace and Freedom Party. California. Hesh Kaplan running for U.S. Congress. 1970.

287. U.S.A. Socialist Workers Party. New York City. Socialist Workers Campaign Committee. *Take us out of Vietnam. Vote for Paul Boutelle, candidate for mayor.* 1969.

288. U.S.A. Republican Party. Youth for Nixon. Richard M. Nixon running for President. 1968.

289. South Korea. Democratic Republican Party. *Fourth Presidential nominating convention of the Democratic Republican Party: Park Chung Hee.* Announcement. 1967.

290. U.S.A. Democratic Party. Pennsylvania. William Sesler running for U.S. Senate, 1970.

291. U.S.A. American Independent Party. George C. Wallace running for President. 1968.

292. U.S.A. Liberal Party. New York City. Committee to Elect the Lindsay Team. John V. Lindsay running for Mayor. 1969.

293. U.S.A. Democratic Party. Hubert H. Humphrey running for President. 1968.

294. U.S.A. Democratic Party. McCarthy for President. Eugene McCarthy campaigning for Democratic Presidential nomination. 1968.

291.

LEADERSHIP FOR AMERICA

GOODLING FOR CONGRESS

LEADERSHIP YOU CAN TRUST

284.

U. S. SENATOR BILL PROXMIRE

285.

HESH KAPLAN 24TH CONGRESSIONAL DISTRICT PEACE AND FREEDOM PARTY

846 CATANIA PLACE CLAREMONT 714.626.6011·213.288.8980 X1657

286.

NIXON'S THE ONE

288.

민주공화당 대통령후보지명 제4년차 전당대회 1967.2.2 장충체육관

전진!

단결!

일꾼중의 일꾼 우리朴正熙총재

289.

YOU CAN COUNT ON BILL SESLER IN THE U.S. SENATE

290.

Vote for New York.

Lindsay, Perrotta, Garelik Vote Liberal—Column "D"

292.

UNITE

WITH HUMPHREY

293.

McCarthy for President

honor...courage...integrity

MCCARTHY FOR PRESIDENT

294.

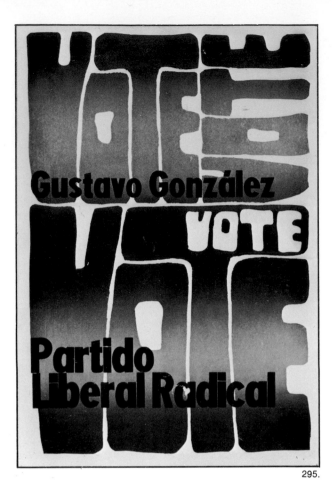

295.

296.

297.

298.

299.

[PUBLIC CITIZEN #1 - PRESIDENT OF THE UNITED STATES IN EXILE - INAUGURATED 3-4-69]

300.

301.

302.						303.

295. Paraguay. Liberal Radical Party. *Vote Gustavo González.*

296. Turkey. Republican People's Party. *Vote the way of Ataturk.* 1970.

297. Mexico. Party of Permanent Revolution (PRI). *Mexico has only one road: Toward revolution. Diaz Ordaz.* (President).

298. Northern Ireland. Labour Party. 1969.

299. Australia. Labor Party. 1968.

300. West Germany. Christian Democratic Union (CDU). *It depends on the Chancellor.* Kurt Georg Kiesinger running for Chancellor. 1969.

301. U.S.A. Peace and Freedom Party. Dick Gregory running for President. 1969.

302. U.S.A. Republican Party. Richard M. Nixon running for President. 1968.

303. U.S.A. Republican Party. New York State. Charles Goodell running for U.S. Senate. 1970.

304. U.S.A. Democratic Party. McCarthy for President. Eugene McCarthy campaigning for Democratic Presidential nomination. 1968.

Give the Presidency back to the people.

McCarthy.

McCarthy for President, 815 17th St., N.W., Washington, D.C., Blair Clark, Campaign Director

304.

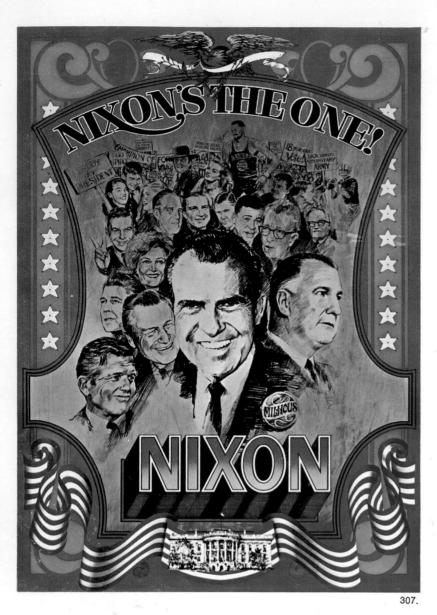

Election Candidates

CANDIDATE
IDENTIFICATION
CONTINUED

305. U.S.A. Democratic Party. New York City. Norman Mailer and Jimmy Breslin running for Democratic nominations for mayor and city council president, promising to make New York City the fifty-first state. 1969.

306. U.S.A. Liberal Party. New York City. Committee to Re-elect John Lindsay. John V. Lindsay running for mayor. 1969.

307. U.S.A. Republican Party. (Final poster design. See page 74 for preliminary sketches). 1968.

308. U.S.A. Liberal Party. New York City. John V. Lindsay running for mayor. Artist: Peter Max. 1969.

307.

306.

305.

311.

312.

313.

314.

316.

318.

320.

317.

321.

323.

324.

325.

326.

97

327. U.S.A. Republican Party. Rockefeller for President Committee. Nelson Rockefeller campaigning for Republican Presidential nomination. 1968.

YESTERDAY'S MEN
(They failed before!)

328. Great Britain. Labour Party. This anti-conservative poster had a great impact in the 196   ons. "Yesterday's men" became a widely quoted catch-phrase. Front row (l. to r.): Sir Alex Douglas-Home; Edward Heath; Lord   back row (l. to r.): Enoch Powell; Iain MacLeod; Reginald Maudling. 1968.

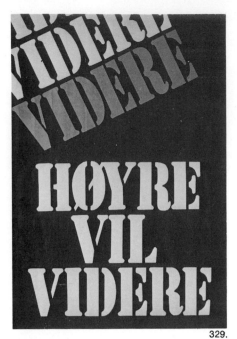

329.

330.

331.

335.

336.

PARTY
IDENTIFICATION
CONTINUED

329. Norway. Conservative Party. *For the future.* 1969.

330. Netherlands. Communist Party. *Row 6.* 1969.

331. Netherlands. People's Party for Freedom and Democracy (VVD). *Row 3: VVD.* 1968.

332. Norway. Liberal Party. *A new government through a strong left.* 1969.

339.

340.

341.

332.

333.

334.

333. Netherlands. Workers Party (PVDA). *Row 1.* 1969.

334. Netherlands. Catholic People's Party (KVP). *Everlasting values. Everlasting welfare. Row 1. KVP.*

335. Iceland. Independent Party. *Row D.*

336. Switzerland. Liberal Party. *Middle-class Liberal: Row 3.* Artist: Celestino Piatti. 1968.

337. India. Congress Party. *Give your vote to Congress Party, for the sake of democracy, good rule, and progress.* 1968.

338. Rumania. United Socialist Front. *We are voting United Socialist Front.*

339. Malaysia. Gerakan Party. *Vote Gerakan.*

340. Italy. Republican Party (PRI). *1946: The republic; 1966: The Republican Party. PRI: A modern left for a society in transition.* Membership card. 1969.

341. Italy. Democratic Socialist Party (PSDI). *Socialism.* 1971.

342. Italy. Republican Party (PRI). *'68: The new line of the Republican Party.* 1968.

343. Italy. Republican Party (PRI). *The clear ideas of the left: PRI.*

344. Italy. Republican Party (PRI). 1969.

337.

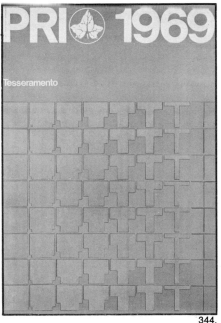

338.

342.

343.

344.

1920 1970

UN PROGRAMME
REALISTE ET NOVATEUR
UN GRAND PARTI
REVOLUTIONNAIRE ET
DEMOCRATIQUE

ADHEREZ AU
PARTI COMMUNISTE
FRANCAIS

PARTI COMMUNISTE FRANÇAIS 44 RUE LE PELETIER PARIS 9

345.

345. France. Communist Party. *1920-1970: A realistic and innovative program. A great party, revolutionary and democratic. Join the French Communist Party.* 1970.

346. Switzerland. Liberal Party. *Think ahead. Vote Liberal. Row 3.* Artist: Celestino Piatti. 1968.

347. Switzerland. Radical Party of Geneva. *It's easier to leave decisions to "them" . . . but Switzerland will go on without us, perhaps against us . . . so vote . . . choose responsibility, progress, liberty — that is, the Radical Party,* 1968.

348. France. Communist Party. *For your future, for the future of France. Have a dialogue with the Communists.* 1968.

349. Sweden. People's Party. *We need a change. The People's Party will get results.* 1968.

350. Rumania. United Socialist Front. *We vote for well-being and peace.*

351. Rumania. United Socialist Front. *Vote March 2.*

352. Sweden. Christian Democratic Union (KDS).

353. Sweden. Social Democratic Party. *Work, Security, Development.* 1968.

354. Sweden. Christian Democratic Union (KDS). *Think new! Vote KDS!* 1969.

355. Great Britain. Liberal Party .

346.

347.

348.

349.

350.

351.

352.

353.

354.

355.

356.

357.

358.

359.

360.

361.

PARTY
IDENTIFICATION
CONTINUED

356. Italy. Republican Party. *We are a republic. Vote Republican.*

357. Netherlands. Workers Party (PVDA). 1968. 1969.

358. Malaysia. Gerakan Party. *Vote Gerakan.*

359. Rumania. United Socialist Front. *Vote for socialism and peace.*

360. Malaysia. Alliance Party.

361. West Germany. Social Democratic Party (SPD). *Participate. Become a member.* 1970.

362. Great Britain. Liberal Party. 1969.

363 Norway Conservative Party. *Party of the future!* 1968.

362.

363

Group Appeals

Group appeals can be broad (to citizens generally) or more narrow and specific (such as the appeals, shown here, to the family, workers, youth, women, the aged, and so forth).

365.

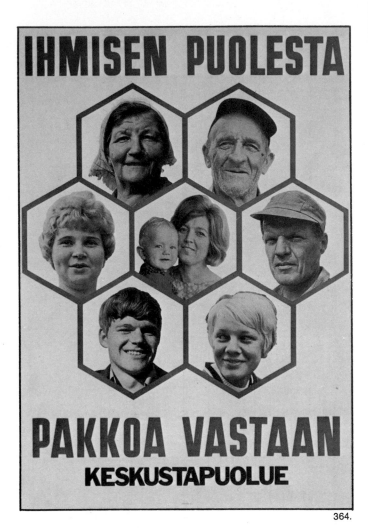

364.

THE PEOPLE

364. Finland. Center Party. *For each individual, against compulsion.* 1968.

365. Australia. Labor Party. 1968.

366. Italy. Democratic Socialist Party. *I am a Roman citizen. I want prosperity and peace, and I want better government in Rome. I will vote Democratic Socialist.* 1971.

367. Denmark. Conservative People's Party. *This time.* 1968.

368. India. Congress Party. *Greetings! For progress and prosperity for youth, farmers, and the state of Haryana, the victory of democracy, congress, and the two yoked bullocks: Vote Congress.* 1969.

369. India. Congress Party. 1968.

370. Great Britain. Liberal Party. 1970.

371. U.S.A. League of Women Voters.

372. Great Britain. Liberal Party. 1970.

373. U.S.A. Nelson Rockefeller campaigning for the Republican Presidential nomination. 1968.

374. South Korea. Democratic Republican Party. *The support of our people. Let us flourish, let us drive, because we have the support of our people.* 1969.

366.

367.

368.

369.

370.

372.

VOTE POWER

Get the Facts
Know the Candidates
Register-Vote
Get Action

Call The League of Women Voters

371.

PEOPLE FOR ROCKEFELLER

373.

이 국민의 지지를
번영으로 몰아가자

민주공화당임시전당대회
1969. 8. 30

374.

THE FAMILY

Muriel Humphrey

375.

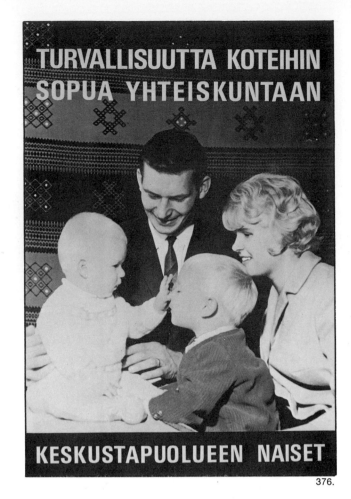

TURVALLISUUTTA KOTEIHIN
SOPUA YHTEISKUNTAAN

KESKUSTAPUOLUEEN NAISET

376.

people with responsibilities vote
Conservative

ACTION not words

377.

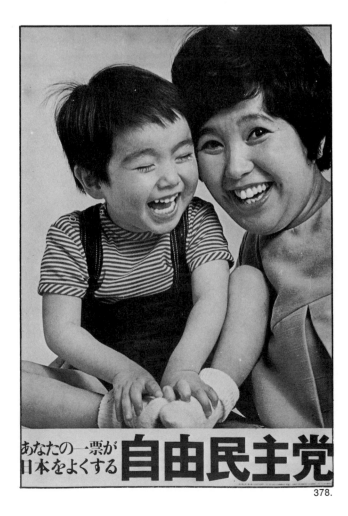

あなたの一票が
日本をよくする 自由民主党

378.

COMME VOUS, NOUS PENSONS D'ABORD A EUX

fédération
DE LA GAUCHE DÉMOCRATE ET SOCIALISTE

379.

CSU Volksbegehren
ab 16. Oktober bis 13. November 1967

nur noch
eine Schule
für alle
Kinder

die **Christliche Volksschule**

380.

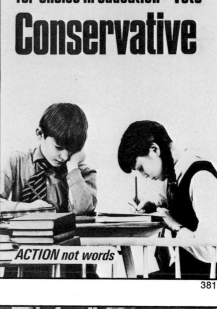

for choice in education — vote
Conservative

ACTION not words

381.

think:
of your
children

VOTE
NDP

382.

KOKOOMUS

varma valinta

383.

This family pays
too much income tax.

Britain would be better off
with the Conservatives

384.

375. U.S.A. Hubert Humphrey campaigning for the Democratic Presidential nomination. Muriel Humphrey, the candidate's wife. 1968.

376. Finland. Women of the Center Party. *Safety in the home. Cooperation in society.* 1968.

377. Great Britain. Conservative Party. 1970.

378. Japan. Liberal Democratic Party. *Your vote will improve Japan.* 1968.

379. France. Federation of the Democratic and Socialist Left. *Like you, we think first of them.* 1967.

380. West Germany. Christian Socialist Union (CSU). *Only one school for all children: The Christian "Volksschule."* 1967.

381. Great Britain. Conservative Party. 1970.

382. Canada. New Democratic Party (NDP). 1969.

383. Finland. Conservative Party. *A secure choice.* 1968.

384. Great Britain. Conservative Party. 1970.

385. Canada. New Democratic Party (NDP). 1968.

think:
of the benefits
of full
employment

VOTE
NDP

385.

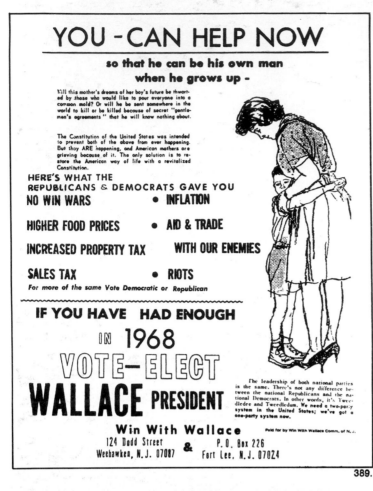

389.

387.

388.

386.

386. Norway. Conservative Party. *For the future.* 1968.
387. Japan. Socialist Party. *A clean and peaceful life.* 1967-68.
388. Great Britain. Conservative Party. 1970.
389. U.S.A. American Independent Party. Presidential election, candidate George Wallace, 1968.
390. New Zealand. Labour Party. 1968.
391. Japan. Socialist Party. *Give this child peace.* 1968.

390.

この子に平和を！

日本社会党

WORKERS AND FARMERS

392.

393.

394.

395.

396.

pour
les petits et moyens paysans
victimes de la politique
du gouvernement...

LE PARTI
COMMUNISTE
FRANÇAIS
propose:
• la priorité pour l'achat et
  la location des terres disponibles
• une juste rémunération de leur travail
• une aide spéciale aux plus défavorisés
• l'amélioration des lois sociales
• un soutien plus important à la coopération

FAITES LUI CONFIANCE
SOUTENEZ SON ACTION

397.

for responsible trade unions—vote
Conservative

ACTION not words

398.

contre
le pouvoir patronal,
organisons le
contrôle ouvrier

PSU
81 rue Mademoiselle-Paris 15

400.

401.

402.

403.

404.

YOUTH

401. Italy. Christian Democratic Party. *My vote is decisive.* 1969.

402. Italy. Republican Party (Youth Federation). Announcement of meeting of Mezzogiorno Giovani ("Young South"), a congress promoted by the Federation of Young Republicans. 1968.

403. Austria. Freedom Party (FPO). *Our responsibility: "More understanding for youth. More rights for women and mothers. More heart for our old people."* 1967.

404. Italy. Christian Democratic Party (DC). *Sports of Youth. Free and strong.*

405. Italy. Republican Party (Youth Federation). *The left and the student movement: A debate organized by the Federation of Young Republicans.* Announcement. 1968.

406. India. Congress Party. *Youth be careful: Ministers who change their loyalties divide the country. Vote Congress.*

407. Austria. Communist Party. *Don't vote old hat. Young people vote Communist.* 1968.

408. Austria. People's Party (OVP). *Young Generation for Vienna.* 1968.

409. Italy. Democratic Socialist Party. *I am a Roman girl. This year I will vote for the first time. I will vote Democratic Socialist.* 1971.

410. Australia. Labor Party. 1968.

411. Sweden. Liberal Party. *Vote — Young.* 1968.

405.

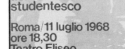

406.

407.

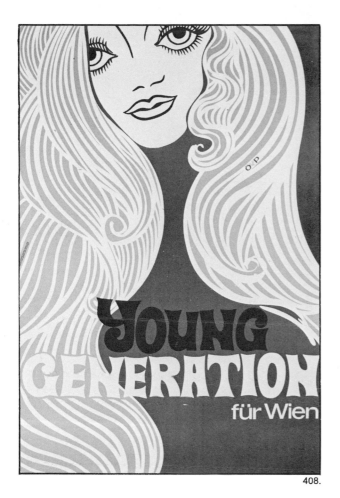

408.

409.

410.

411.

412.

414.

415.

413.

416.

417.

412. Great Britain. Conservative Party. 1970.

413. Netherlands. *For us, a woman is not a number!* 1970.

414. Finland. Social Democratic Party. *Along a firm road.* 1969.

415. Finland. Center Party. *Peace, safety, justice.* 1968.

416. Italy. Democratic Socialist Party. *I am a Roman schoolboy. I want to go to a modern school without double sessions. So my mother and father will vote Democratic Socialist.* 1971.

417. Norway. *Build up with youth.*

Election Campaign Issues

Interestingly, campaign issues around the world are quite similar.

Have you ever wondered just where this country <u>is</u> <u>going</u>?

We <u>worry</u> about it all the time.

NDP

THE <u>NEW</u> PARTY!

418.

Let's give the old parties a well-deserved rest.

This country needs it.

NDP

THE <u>ENERGETIC</u> PARTY

419.

420.

"WE ARE BETTER. THEY ARE BAD."

418. Canada. New Democratic Party (NDP). 1969.
419. Canada. New Democratic Party (NDP). 1969.
420. Finland. Conservative Party. *Think: Things can't continue like this.* 1968.
421. Austria. People's Party (OVP). *The OVP mandate or the Socialist Party (SPO) mandate. The first of March (voting day) is important.*
422. Great Britain. Conservative Party. 1968.
423. Sweden. Conservative Party. *Ten new Conservative seats will give you a better government.* 1968.
424. Great Britain. Liberal Party. Harold Wilson (Labour Party) and Edward Heath (Conservative Party). The implication is that there is no difference between the two major candidates. 1970.

85 oder 85
ÖVP Mandate   SPÖ Mandate

Darum geht es am 1. März

421.

CONSERVATIVES WILL PUT BRITAIN BACK ON HER FEET

422.

Det är 10 nya högermandat som ska ge Dig en bättre regering Högerpartiet

423.

Which Twin is the Tory

only LIBERAL means PROGRESS

424.

425.

426.

427.

"WE ARE BETTER. THEY ARE BAD."
CONTINUED

425. Norway. Conservative People's Party. *No to the Socialist plurality. Vote row C.* 1968.

426. Ireland. Labour Party. 1970.

427. Ireland. Labour Party. 1970.

428. France. Communist League. *Poher . . . a braggart. Pompidou . . . an idiot. Abstain.* Presidential elections, 1969.

429. Italy. Republican Party (PRI). *Stop. A firm stand in the confusion.*

430. Great Britain. Conservative Party. 1970.

431. India. Congress Party. *Beware of them: These party-changers are a danger to the stability of democracy and government. For a strong government and prosperity, vote Congress.* 1968.

428.

429.

430.

431.

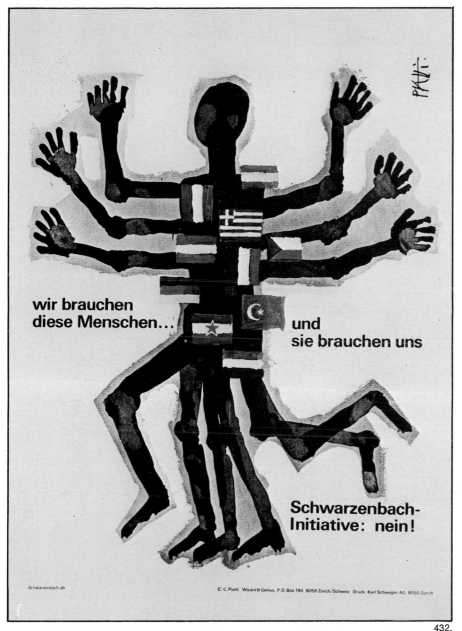

wir brauchen
diese Menschen…

und
sie brauchen uns

Schwarzenbach-
Initiative: nein!

432.

fight rising prices—vote
Conservative

ACTION not words

433.

432. Switzerland. *We need these men . . . and they need us. Urging vote against limiting immigration to Switzerland.* Artist: C. Piatti. 1971.

433. Great Britain. A Conservative Party. 1969.

434. Austria. Freedom Party (RPO). *A complete success: Freedom of conscience, freedom of employment, a free economy.* 1967.

435. Luxembourg. Socialist Party. *Your francs should not be worth less. Vote Socialist and prevent price increases.*

30% aller Stimmen

EIN VOLLER ERFOLG

DEN
FREIHEITLICHEN
DIE ZUKUNFT

Freiheitlicher Gesinnung
Freiheitlicher Arbeit
Freiheitlicher Gemeinschaft

FPÖ

Das zeigten die Hochschulwahlen 1967

434.

dein Franken
darf nicht kleiner
werden

deshalb mit den
Sozialisten
gegen die
Preistreiberei!

435.

Vote Conservative and together we'll keep things moving

436.

IMPOTS ÉCRASANTS

pour les salariés, pensionnés et retraités

CADEAUX

pour les grandes sociétés capitalistes

Avec le **PCF** PARTI COMMUNISTE FRANÇAIS

Exigez une

RÉFORME DÉMOCRATIQUE DE LA FISCALITÉ

P.C.F. 44, RUE LE PELETIER, PARIS-IX

437.

1964 .... **£15**
1969 .... **£25**

Britain was better off with the Conservatives

438.

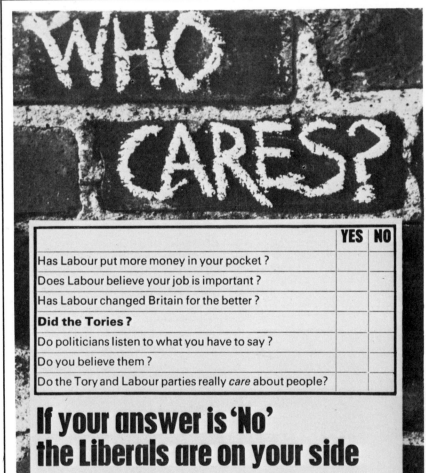

	YES	NO
Has Labour put more money in your pocket ?		
Does Labour believe your job is important ?		
Has Labour changed Britain for the better ?		
Did the Tories ?		
Do politicians listen to what you have to say ?		
Do you believe them ?		
Do the Tory and Labour parties really *care* about people?		

If your answer is 'No' the Liberals are on your side

It's *your* country, not the politicians! It's *your* voice that should really count. But at present it's *you* who always loses out in the bungling and drift of every Tory and Labour Government since the war.

Wilson or Heath ? What's the difference ? They're both a couple of Tories. Both put politics before people. Both put power before progress.

LIBERALS PUT PEOPLE FIRST

439.

LE PARTI COMMUNISTE FRANÇAIS agit pour
la réduction des dépenses improductives
la suppression des cadeaux aux grands capitalistes

l'augmentation des crédits aux collectivités locales: pour l'enseignement, le logement, la santé, le sport, les activités culturelles, la voirie- *soutenez son action*

440.

THE ECONOMY
CONTINUED

436. Great Britain. Conservative Party. 1970.

437. France. Communist Party (PCF). *Crushing taxes for salaries, pensions, retirement funds. Favors to large capitalist corporations. With PCF, demand a democratic reform of fiscal policy.* 1969.

438. Great Britain. Conservative Party. 1969.

439. Great Britain. Liberal Party.

440. France. Communist Party. *The French Communist campaigns for the reduction of unproductive expenditures, the elimination of favors to big capitalists, the increase of credit to local groups for teaching, housing, health, sports, cultural activities, transportation facilities. Support the party's action.* 1969.

441. France. Socialist Party. *Against the profi-*

441.

442.

443.

444.

teers, with the Socialist Party, take your city in hand. 1971.

442. Denmark. Liberal Party. *Order in the Danish economy — row D*. 1968.

443. Great Britain. Conservative Party. 1969.

444. U.S.A. American Independent Party. *Win with Wallace*. George C. Wallace running for President. 1968.

445. Switzerland. Radical Democratic Party of Fribourg. *The Radical Party has ensured the independence and prosperity of Switzerland for over a century. Today, as yesterday, it is ready to assume its responsibility and to guide the country's future, according to the principles of freedom and democracy to which we owe our strength and individuality. Its only goal is to promote the well-being of the people. Have confidence in it.* 1968.

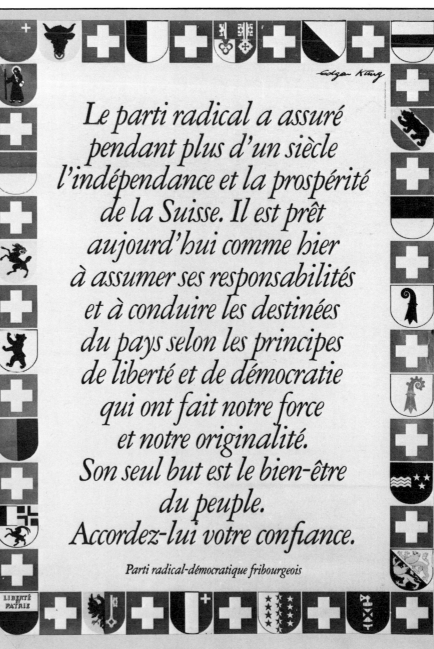

445.

446. France. United Socialist Party (PSU). *Are you dependent on those who colonize French Industry? Fight NATO, which links France to American Imperialism.* 1969.

447. Austria. Freedom Party (FPO). *The People's Party (OVP) makes debts. The Socialists do nothing. Both are endangering the economy and employment. FPO is the way out.* Picture of a cracked one-schilling piece. 1967.

448. France. Communist Party. *Capitalist profits, an obstacle to social progress, bankrupt the nation. Support the French Communist Party, party of the working class, the people, and the nation.* 1969.

449. Austria. Freedom Party (FPO). *The FPO repeats: The People's Party (OVP) election promises, there is no progress on the question of the Common Market. Therefore: higher prices, continuing housing shortages, and unemployment.* 1967.

450. New Guyana. People's Progressive Party (PPP). 1969.

451. U.S.A. American Independent Party. *Win with Wallace.* George C. Wallace running for President. 1968.

452.

453.

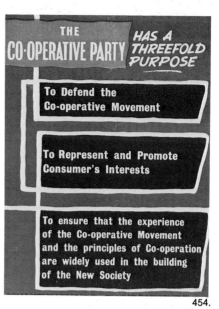

454.

Election Campaign Issues

CONSUMER PROTECTION

452. Canada. New Democratic Party (NDP). 1969.
453. Great Britain. Co-operative Party. 1969.
454. Great Britain. Co-operative Party. 1969.
455. Finland. Center Party. *More inexpensive public housing.* 1968.
456. Great Britain. Co-operative Party. 1969.
457. Great Britain. Co-operative Party. 1969.
458. Great Britain. Co-operative Party. 1969.

455.

456.

457.

458.

REGIONAL INTERESTS

459. Wales.
460. Australia. Labor Party. 1968.
461. Australia. Labor Party. 1968.
462. Cyprus. Democratic National Party. *Annexation (to Greece) is our undying goal.*

459.

460.

LAW AND ORDER

463.

464.

465.

461.

462.

466.

463. U.S.A. American Independent Party. Win with Wallace. George C. Wallace running for President. 1968.

464. Austria. Freedom Party (FPO). *For Europe in freedom and order.* 1967.

465. Austria. Freedom Party (FPO). *Our wish for 1967: Order and clean government in the country.* 1967.

466. Austria. People's Party (OVP). *No crisis with the People's Party. Neutrality, domestic peace, full employment.* 1970.

467. Belgium. United People's Party. *Riots? Or a permanent solution? Freedom through federalism.* 1968.

467.

468.

469.

HEALTH AND EDUCATION

468. Norway. Conservative Party. *The future demands better education now. Vote the party with the future.* 1968.
469. Canada. New Democratic Party (NDP). 1969.
470. Australia. Labor Party. 1968.
471. Italy. Republican Party (PRI). *Reform of medical studies.* Announcement of meeting. 1969.

470.

471.

472.

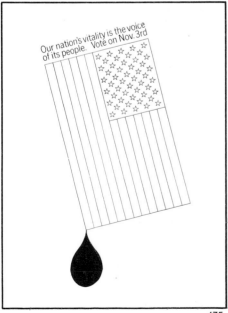

475.

Defend Your Life Style — and Your Life

YOUR LIFE STYLE MEANS YOUR RIGHT TO:
Put what you want in your pipe and smoke it;
Dress the way you want, make love in your
 own way, and to whom you want;
Enjoy your freedom to live your own life,
 as long as you are'nt hurting others.
Your life style is your freedom - Defend it.

But more than your freedom is at stake.
So is your life. The government we have not
only ordered the Chicago police to club us down,
it is also drafting us to be killed in Vietnam.
The government we've got can kill us.

Some guys are skipping to Canada to avoid the
draft. We say it is time for Johnson and Humphrey,
Nixon and Wallace to skip to Canada-- and let
us begin to build an American society worth
living in, and worth raising our kids in.

Register And VOTE

If you will be 21 by November 5th, and if you have lived in New York State for
three months by November 5th, you can register and vote in the general election.

THERE IS A CHOICE. You are'nt stuck with Humphery or Nixon. ELDRIDGE CLEAVER and
JUDY MAGE are running for President and Vice President on the Peace and Freedom
ticket.

In the 19th Congressional District (East Village, Lower Manhattan, and the West
Side) DAVE McREYNOLDS is the Peace and Freedom Candidate for Congress.
He is on the ballot. He needs your help.

Defend your life style and your life. Join the Peace and Freedom Party. Register
to vote. Come out before November 5th to help your candidates. Come out on November 5th to vote for your party. And let us work together after November 5th
to build Peace and Freedom into the political arm of a growing movement.
                    to find the place nearest you to register
                    Phone the Board of Elections 966 4570
                    Registration times are: Sept. 30, Oct. 3 and 4,
                    5:30 to 10:30 PM; Oct. 5, 7:00 AM to 10:30PM.

McREYNOLDS FOR CONGRESS
PEACE AND FREEDOM PARTY
4 BETHUNE ST.
CH 3-9812

474.

MISCELLANEOUS

472. Chile. *For the new Chile, a new university.* 1971.

473. Sweden. Christian Democratic Union (KDS). *What does the election result mean for Christianity's influence on society?*

474. U.S.A. Peace and Freedom Party. 1968.

475. U.S.A. Art Directors' Club of Charlotte, North Carolina. Design: Harry Jacobs. Art: Al Whitley. 1965.

476.

477.

478.

Announcements

Announcement posters do not simply give the basic information of when and where, but often graphically persuade the viewer to participate in the event and be sympathetic to its sponsors' cause. Shown here are samples of posters for Congresses, meetings, rallies, exhibitions, cultural events, and celebrations, as well as political publications. All this is part of the variety and depth of a poster's use in the preparation for an election.

479.

480.

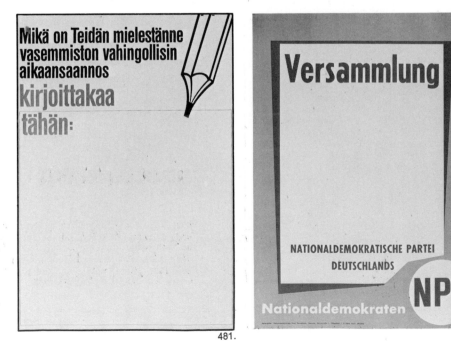

481.

482.

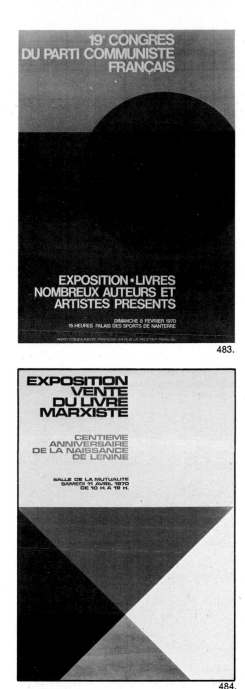

483.

486.

485.

476. Austria. People's Party (OVP). *Exhibition. Think ahead. Keep up with world developments.*

477. Austria. People's Party (OVP). *Invitation. Photography Contest.*

478. Austria. People's Party (OVP). *The state chief will answer your questions.* 1968.

479. Australia. Labor Party. Advertisement for *Trend*, the party magazine. 1968.

480. Chad. Progressive Party (PPT). *Boys and girls, farmers, students and workers, young executives of all levels: The PPT, RDA (Chad section of the African Democratic Assembly), party of unity and progress, invites you to participate in building our nation. . . . The nation will rise from the earth! . . . Your country calls you. . . . . Be strong, be demanding . . . . If you are worthy of your heritage, you will be worthy of liberty.* 1968.

481. Finland. Conservative Party. *Think of the worst failures of the leftist government . . . and write them here:* 1968.

482. West Germany. National Democratic Party (NPD). *Meeting.* 1968.

483. France. Communist Party *19th Congress of the French Communist Party Exhibition. Books. Numerous authors and artists present.* 1970.

484. France. Communist Party. *Exhibition. Sale of Marxist books. One hundredth anniversary of Lenin's birth.* 1970.

485. France. United Socialist Party (PSU). *The PSU speaks: Socialist forum.* 1969.

486. France. Association of Students from Guadeloupe (AGEG), Federation of Black African Students in France (FEANF), and Center for Vietnam Information (CIV). *Anti-Imperialist Meeting. Long live the victorious war of the people of Vietnam. Down with American imperialism and its lackeys. Down with French imperialism and its puppets. Long live the struggle for freedom by the people of the world.* 1971.

Che succede nella politica italiana?

La Malfa
sulle ragioni e le responsabilità della crisi attuale

La politica del PRI
Con una cronistoria degli avvenimenti dal dicembre 1968

**In questa edicola
lire 200**

487.

apres leur 19e congres
que proposent les communistes?
expose de
**georges
marchais**
secretaire général adjoint
du parti communiste francais
sous la présidence de
paul laurent
membre du bureau politique
**au grand
meeting
mardi 24 mar
à la mutualité**
20h.30 24 r. s'victor paris 5e
projection du film 'la vie est a nous'
de jean renoir

488.

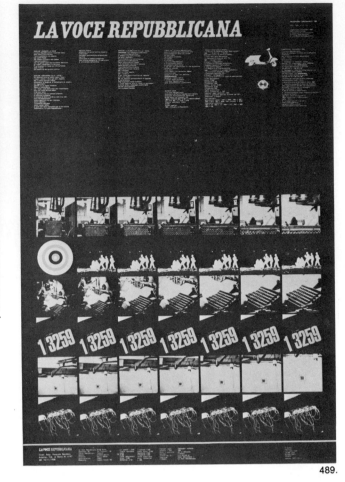

489.

487. Italy. Republican Party (PRI). *What is happening in Italian politics? La Malfa (party president) writes on the reasons and responsibility for the current crisis.* Advertisement for *La politica del PRI* ("The politics of the Republican Party of Italy").

488. France. Communist Party. *After the 19th congress, what does the party have in mind? Georges Marchais explains.* 1969.

489. Italy. Republican Party (PRI). Advertisement for *La Voce Repubblicana,* the party journal.

490. Italy. Republican Party (PRI). *The education policies of the Republican Party for the fifth legislature.*

491. Italy. Christian Democratic Party (DC). *11th National Congress. Ideas, frameworks, proposals of the DC for the renovation of institutions and the democratic development of Italian society.* 1969.

**La politica scolastica
del Partito repubblicano
per la 5ª legislatura**

Pisa 25·26 novembre
Hotel Mediterraneo

490.

idee strutture iniziative della dc per
il rinnovamento delle istituzioni e lo
sviluppo democratico della società italiana

LIBERTAS

**XI CONGRESSO NAZIONALE
DELLA DEMOCRAZIA CRISTIANA**
ROMA 27-30 GIUGNO 1969

491.

492.

493.

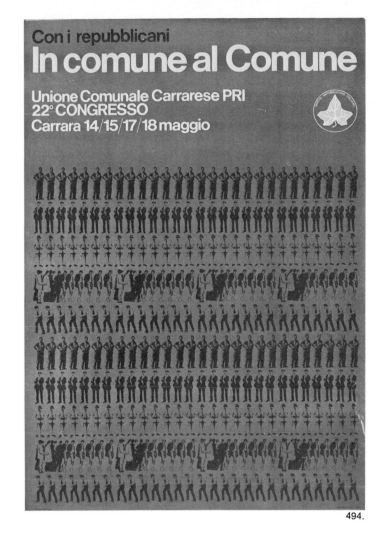

494.

492. 493. Italy. Christian Democratic Party (DC). Advertisements for *Il Punto*, the party journal: Reprints of pages.

494. Italy. Republican Party (PRI). *In step with the community. 22nd Congress.*

495. Italy. Italian Labor Union (UIL). 5th National Congress. *A strong union for a just society.*

496. Italy. Republican Party (PRI). *What is happening in the capital?* (Topic to be discussed at a meeting.)

497. Great Britain. Liberal Party. 1970.

495.

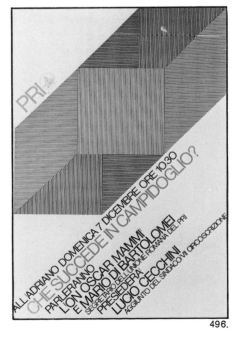

496.

497.

498.

499.

500.

501.

502.

503.

504.

505.

506.

6.25 상기하여

싸우면서
건설하자!

공보부

507.

ANNOUNCEMENTS CONTINUED

498. Netherlands. Announcement of Truth Festival. 1968.

499. Italy. National Democratic Organization for Social Action (ENDAS). *10th National Congress, Naples.* 1969.

500. Malagasy Republic (Madagascar). Social Democratic Party (PSD).

501. South Korea. *Celebration of victory from Japanese colonial rule.*

502. Poland. Peasant Holiday Celebration Committee. *Peasant Holiday.* 1968.

503. Poland. Peasant Holiday Celebration Committee. *Celebration of the peasant holiday will take place on . . . . Program will be . . . .* 1969.

504. Poland. Peasant Holiday Celebration Committee. *Peasant Holiday.* 1966.

505. Poland. Agrarian Party (ZSL). *5th Congress.* 1969.

506. Poland. Agrarian Party (ZSL). *5th Congress.* 1969.

507. South Korea. *Celebration of the victory over the North.*

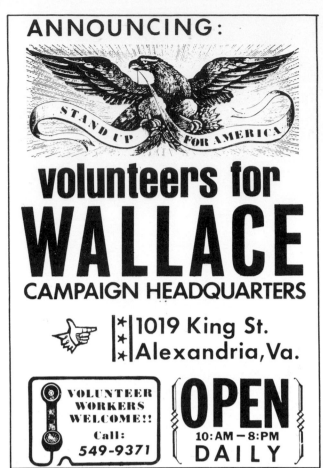

508. U.S.A. American Independent Party. George C. Wallace running for President. 1968.

509. U.S.A. Students for a Democratic Society. 1969.

512. U.S.A. New York Democratic Coalition. Democrats protest the Vietnam War, addressing their complaints to New York State governor Nelson Rockefeller. 1970.

513. U.S.A. 1970.

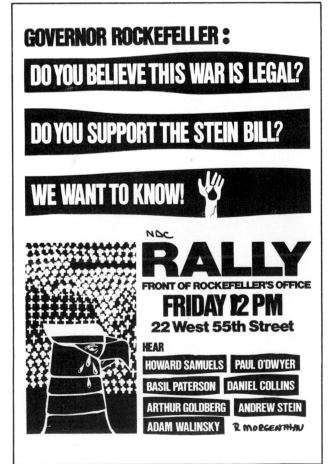

510. U.S.A. Student Mobilization Committee. Newspaper insert. 1970.

511. Rumania. Communist Party. *10th Congress.* 1969.

514.

515.

514. Poland. Peasant Holiday Celebration Committee. *Celebration of the peasant holiday will take place on .... Program will be .... 1968.*

515. U.S.A. Republican Party. Richard M. Nixon running for President. 1968.

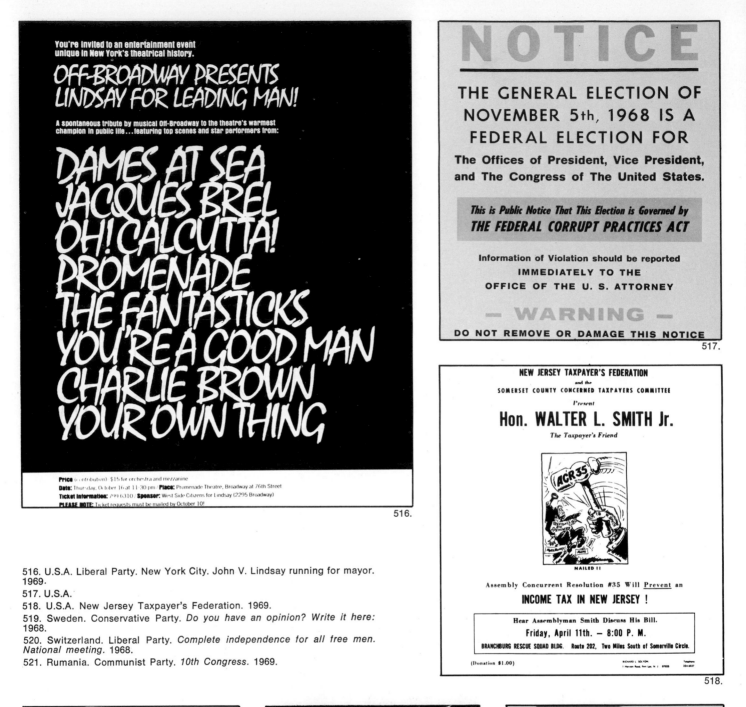

You're invited to an entertainment event unique in New York's theatrical history.

OFF-BROADWAY PRESENTS LINDSAY FOR LEADING MAN!

A spontaneous tribute by musical Off-Broadway to the theatre's warmest champion in public life...featuring top scenes and star performers from:

DAMES AT SEA
JACQUES BREL
OH! CALCUTTA!
PROMENADE
THE FANTASTICKS
YOU'RE A GOOD MAN
CHARLIE BROWN
YOUR OWN THING

Price (contribution): $15 for orchestra and mezzanine
Date: Thursday, October 16 at 11:30 pm. **Place:** Promenade Theatre, Broadway at 76th Street
Ticket Information: 799-6310. **Sponsor:** West Side Citizens for Lindsay (2295 Broadway)
PLEASE NOTE: Ticket requests must be mailed by October 10!

516.

NOTICE

THE GENERAL ELECTION OF NOVEMBER 5th, 1968 IS A FEDERAL ELECTION FOR

The Offices of President, Vice President, and The Congress of The United States.

This is Public Notice That This Election is Governed by
THE FEDERAL CORRUPT PRACTICES ACT

Information of Violation should be reported
**IMMEDIATELY TO THE
OFFICE OF THE U. S. ATTORNEY**

— WARNING —
DO NOT REMOVE OR DAMAGE THIS NOTICE

517.

516. U.S.A. Liberal Party. New York City. John V. Lindsay running for mayor. 1969.
517. U.S.A.
518. U.S.A. New Jersey Taxpayer's Federation. 1969.
519. Sweden. Conservative Party. *Do you have an opinion? Write it here:* 1968.
520. Switzerland. Liberal Party. *Complete independence for all free men. National meeting.* 1968.
521. Rumania. Communist Party. *10th Congress.* 1969.

NEW JERSEY TAXPAYER'S FEDERATION
and the
SOMERSET COUNTY CONCERNED TAXPAYERS COMMITTEE
Present

Hon. WALTER L. SMITH Jr.

The Taxpayer's Friend

Assembly Concurrent Resolution #35 Will <u>Prevent</u> an
INCOME TAX IN NEW JERSEY !

Hear Assemblyman Smith Discuss His Bill.
Friday, April 11th. — 8:00 P. M.
BRANCHBURG RESCUE SQUAD BLDG.   Route 202, Two Miles South of Somerville Circle.

(Donation $1.00)

518.

519.

520.

521.

SECTION. II.
Major Political Events

It is revealing how much our consciousness of recent history has been shaped by the posters which these events have generated. Almost all newsworthy happenings have posters associated with them. This section presents some of these events.

522. China. On behalf of our great leader Mao, fight gloriously. *On behalf of the great socialist bloc, fight gloriously.* 1970.

523. China. *Chairman Mao, who is the reddest, is now with us.*

524. China. *The strong central core that leads us in our occupations is the Communist Party. The ideological base that guides us in our thought is Marxism-Leninism. 1967.*

525. China. *Establish a new standard of merit on behalf of the people's achievements. 1967.*

The Cultural Revolution in China. 1966-1969

伟大的导师 伟大的领袖 伟大的统帅 伟大的舵手

毛主席万岁 万万岁

526.

527.

528.

从政治上思想上理伧上彻底批倒批臭中国的赫鲁晓夫

529.

走大寨之路
ZOU DA ZHAI ZHI LU

530.

不管敌机白天来黑
夜来高空来低空来 来者必歼!
LAI ZHE BI JIAN

531.

526. China. Mao Tse-tung.

527. China. Mao Tse-tung.

528. China. *Chairman Mao is the red sun in the East.*

529. China. *In the political sphere, ideological sphere, thoroughly criticize China's Khrushchev.* 1967.

530. China. *Follow the path* (set forth by Ta Chai collective).

531. China. *Whether they fly by day or night, whether they fly high or low, the enemy planes must be wiped out.*

我们的文学艺术都是为人民大众的，首先是为工农兵的，为工农兵而创作，为工农兵所利用的。

毛泽东
（在延安文艺座谈会上的讲话）

532.

生命不息，冲锋不止
CHARGE THE ENEMY TO THE LAST BREATH

533.

要使文艺很好地成为整个革命机器的一个组成部分，作为团结人民、教育人民、打击敌人、消灭敌人的有力的武器，帮助人民同心同德地和敌人作斗争。

毛泽东
（在延安文艺座谈会上的讲话）

534.

532. China. "Art and literature are for the people, among whom the workers, farmers, and soldiers are the most respected."—Mao Tse-tung.

533. China.

534. China. "We must make literature and art a component of the entire revolutionary machine, use it as a powerful weapon in uniting the people, attacking the enemy, and destroying the enemy."—Mao Tse-tung. Quotation taken from a speech by Mao Tse-tung at a panel discussion on literature and art at Yon-an Province.

535. China. Resolutely support the American people in their opposition to American aggression in Vietnam.

536. China. Chairman Mao Tse-tung is the greatest Marxist-Leninist of the present day. Comrade Mao Tse-tung brilliantly and creatively inherited, defended, and advanced Marxism-Leninism. . . . When imperialism is moving toward collapse, socialism is approaching world-wide victory.

537. China. We are determined to liberate Taiwan. 1967.

538. China. The people's soldiers are the base for victory.

539. China. Long Live the Great Unity of the Working People of the World!

540. China. Keep the country in Heart and the whole world in Mind.

541. China.

堅決支持美國人民 反对美帝国主义侵略越南
JIAN JUE ZHI CHI MEI GUO REN MIN FAN DUI MEI DI GUO ZHU YI QIN LÜE YUE NAN

535.

536.

一定要解放台湾
We are determined to liberate Taiwan!
Nous libérerons Taiwan!
Wir werden Taiwan unbedingt befreien!

537.

兵民是胜利之本

538.

全世界劳动人民
大团结万岁

Long Live the Great Unity of the Working People of the World!
Vive la grande unité des peuples travailleurs du monde entier!
¡Viva la gran unidad de los pueblos trabajadores del mundo!

QUAN SHI JIE LAO DONG REN MIN DA TUAN JIE WAN SUI

539.

胸怀祖国
放眼世界

Keep the Country in Heart and the Whole World in Mind!
Avec la patrie dans le cœur et le monde entier pour horizon!
Das Vaterland im Herzen tragen, den Blick auf die ganze Welt richten!

540.

到工农兵群众中去 到火热的斗争中去
Go Among the Workers, Peasants and Soldiers and into the Thick of Struggle!
Allons parmi les ouvriers, paysans et soldats! Jetons-nous dans la lutte ardente!
Unter die Massen der Arbeiter, Bauern und Soldaten gehen, zu flammendem Kampf gehen!

541.

Greek Junto. April, 1967.

542. Great Britain. International Union of Students. 1970.

543. U.S.A. Announcement. 1970.

544. France. United Socialist Party (PSU). *Are you in agreement with those who support the Greek colonels? Fight against NATO, which ties France to American imperialism.* 1969.

545. Great Britain. International Union of Students. 1970.

144

קופל גורבינוק

יום העצמאות תשל"א

הועדה לחגיגות יום העצמאות · מרכז הסברה · הוצאת המדפיס הממשלתי · הדפסה דפוס יפת בע"מ

546. Israel. *Independence Day*, 1971.

Arab-Israeli Conflict. June, 1967

هذا طريقي في الكفاح
فيا أخي أتمم كفاحي

547.

COME HOME TO ISRAEL

548.

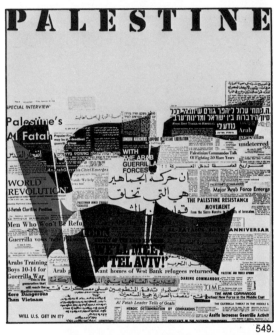

PALESTINE

549.

PALESTINE

Know Your Brothers
Show Your Revolutionary Solidarity

AL-FATEH
Revolution
Until Victory

550.

יום העצמאות תשל״ו

551.

552.

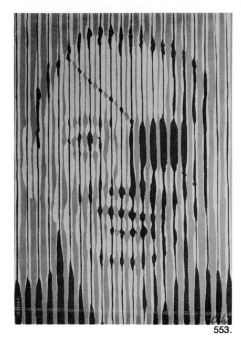

553.

554.

555.

Arab-Israeli Conflict. 1967-71.

547. Palestine Liberation Movement. *This is my way in the battle, and, oh, my brother, I will complete the defense.*

548. Israel. State of Immigration Office. 1970.

549. U.S.A.

550. U.S.A.

551. Israel. *Independence Day 1970.*

552. Israel. *Shalom.* Artist: Dan Reisinger. 1970.

553. Israel. Moshe Dayan. Artist: Bahot. 1970.

554. Israel. State of Israel Immigration Office. *From immigrant to immigrant, our strength increases.*

555. Israel. *Jerusalem (above). 20 years of Israeli independence.* 1968.

556. The Democratic Front for the Liberation of Palestine. 1949.

557. Palestine Liberation Movement.

558. France. Marxist Revolutionary League, and others. *Why the Palestinian Resistance?* Announcement. 1970.

559. U.S.A. Announcement. 1970.

556.

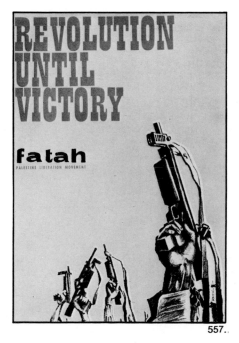

557.

558.

559.

560. Israel. *Independence Day* 1970.

Arab-Israeli Conflict. June, 1967

Assassination of Che Guevara. October, 1967.

561. Cuba. *1868-1968: A century of struggle*.1968.

562. Cuba. *Ever onward to victory*. 1970.

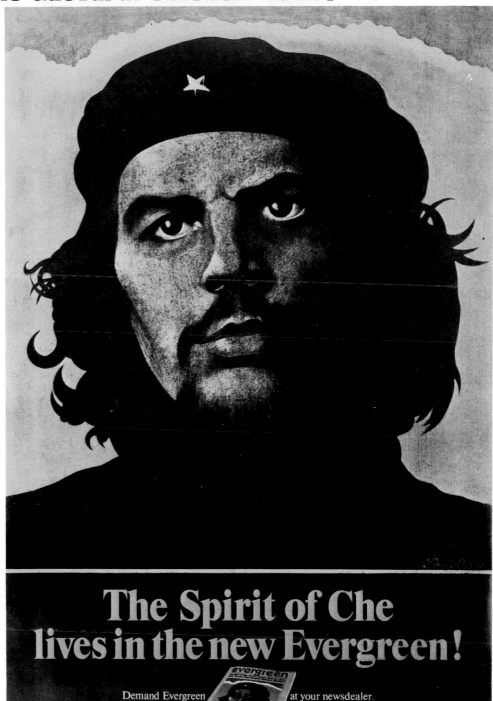

The Spirit of Che lives in the new Evergreen!

Demand Evergreen at your newsdealer.

563. U.S.A. Advertisement for the magazine *Evergreen Review*. 1968.

564.

HASTA LA VICTORIA SIEMPRE

565.

DEL 8 AL 28 DE OCTUBRE

JOR
NADA
NACIO
NAL
GUE
RRI
LLERA

566.

OTHER HANDS WILL TAKE UP THE WEAPONS.

ICAP

567.

OTHER HANDS WILL TAKE UP THE WEAPONS.

ICAP

568.

569.

570.

564. Cuba. OSPAAAL. 1968.
565. Canada. Fair Play for Cuba Committee. *Ever onward toward victory.* 1967.
566. Cuba. *National Guerrilla* Day. 1968.
567. Cuba. Cuban Institute for Friendship with Foreign Peoples (ICAP). 1971.
568. Cuba. Cuban Institute for Friendship with Foreign Peoples. (ICAP).
569. Cuba. Cuban Institute for Friendship with Foreign Peoples (ICAP).
"*Wherever death may surprise us, let it be welcome if our battle cry has reached even one receptive ear and another hand reaches out to take up our arms.*"
Che. 1970.
570. Cuba. Organization of Latin American Students. 1968.
571. U.S.A. Young Socialist Alliance. 1968.
572. Cuba. *The heroic guerrilla. 1967: 10th anniversary of the revolution.* 1970.

Wherever death may surprise us,
let it be welcome if our battle cry
has reached even one receptive ear
and another hand reaches out
to take up our arms...
— Che

571.

1967
GUERRILLERO HEROICO
DECIMO ANIVERSARIO DEL TRIUNFO DE LA REBELION

572.

Assassination of Martin Luther King. April, 1968.

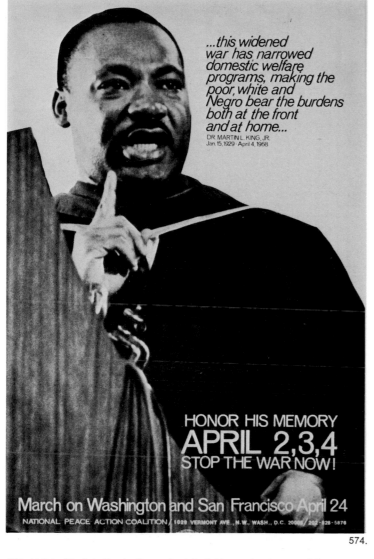

...this widened
war has narrowed
domestic welfare
programs, making the
poor, white and
Negro bear the burdens
both at the front
and at home...
DR. MARTIN L. KING, JR.
Jan. 15, 1929 - April 4, 1968

HONOR HIS MEMORY
APRIL 2,3,4
STOP THE WAR NOW!

March on Washington and San Francisco April 24
NATIONAL PEACE ACTION COALITION / 1029 VERMONT AVE., N.W., WASH., D.C. 20005 / 202-828-5876

574.

LOS ANGELES · MEMPHIS · MONTGOMERY · MIAMI
ATLANTA · BIRMINGHAM · DALLAS · DETROIT · JACKSON · LITTLE ROCK
NEW ORLEANS · NEW YORK · RICHMOND · SELMA · WASHINGTON, D.C. · OSLO

"If a man hasn't found something he will die for, he isn't fit to live."

Dr. Martin Luther King, Jr. 1929-1968 · In Memoriam

575.

573. U.S.A. Starfish Productions. A civil rights poster prompted by King's death.

574. U.S.A. National Peace Action Coalition.

575. U.S.A. Southern Christian Leadership Conference. 1968.

576. U.S.A.

577. U.S.A. "In memoriam." 1968.

I have a dream...

576.

577.

579.

Paris May Revolt. May, 1968.

578, 579, 580, 581, 582. Political posters in Paris, May, 1968.

580.

581.

582.

LA LUTTE CONTINUE

583.

NOUS IRONS JUSQU'AU BOUT

"WE WILL GO ALL THE WAY"—French revolutionary poster by L'Ecole des Beaux Arts
Published in the U.S. by the YOUNG SOCIALIST ALLIANCE in solidarity with the French workers and students

584.

INFORMATION LIBRE

585.

nous sommes le pouvoir

586.

583. France. *The fight goes on.*

584. U.S.A. Young Socialist Alliance. *We'll go all the way.* Reprint of a French student poster. 1968.

585. France. *Uncensored information.*

586. France. *We are the power.*

587. France. *Frontiers-Repression.*

588. France. *Long live the struggle of the small worker.*

589. France. *"You are the guerilla fighting against the conditioned death they wish to sell you under the name of the future."* — Cortazar.

FRONTIÈRES REPRESSION

587.

VIVE LA LUTTE
DES TRAVAILLEURS
DANS LES
PETITES
ENTREPRISES

588.

Vous êtes la guérrilla contre la mort climatisée qu'on veut vous vendre sous le nom d'avenir. Cortázar

589.

155

590.

591.

592.

593.

SALAIRES LEGERS

CHARS LOURDS

594.

590. France. *We must prevent the worm of power from devouring the fruit and destroying the garden.*

591. France. *Yes! To occupied factories.*

592. France. *The police speak to you every evening at 8:00* (ORTF: French national radio and television).

593. France. *"Chienlit" parade.* Paraphrasing De Gaulle.

594. France. *Light salaries . . . heavy tanks.*

595. France. French parliament (initials of the parties). *Power of the people.*

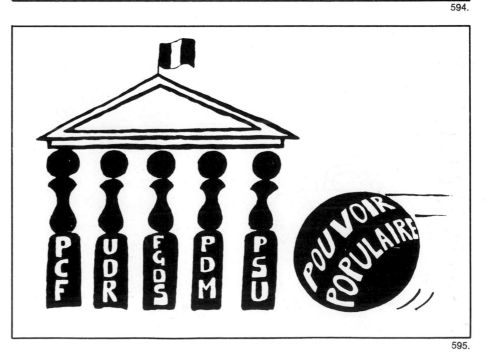

595.

596.

597.

598.

599.

600.

601.

596. France. *Beware of informers!*
597. France. CRS-SS. (Companie Républicaine de Sécurité.) 1968.
598. France. *The police post themselves in the Beaux-Arts. The Beaux-Arts sticks posters in the streets.*
599. France. *The time of cherries.*
600. France.
601. France. *Me.* Caricature of De Gaulle.

602.

603.

604.

605.

606.

607.

608.

609.

Paris May Revolt. May, 1968.

CONTINUED

602. France. Atelier Populaire de Marseille. *Examinations in order. "Admitted: legal unemployment."*

603. France. Atelier Populaire de Marseille. *No to the police state. Against repression in silence. Organize into neighborhood action committees.*

604. France. *Establishment action . . . fascist vermin.*

605. France. Atelier Populaire de Marseille. *To maintain low salaries, capitalism needs unemployment. Soon 700,000 unemployed.*

606. France. Atelier Populaire de Marseille. *Buy more . . . they (capitalists) profit more. Expansion is for them.*

607. France. Atelier Populaire de Marseille. Action Committee of Workers and Students. *Against capitalist exploitation, our fight goes on.*

608. France. Atelier Populaire de Marseille. *We participate. They choose.*

609. France. *The vote doesn't change anything. The fight goes on . . . against official medicine.*

610. France. *No to Gaullist fascism.*

610.

Resurrection City.
June, 1968.

611. U.S.A. Southern Christian Leadership Conference (SCLC).

612. U.S.A. Southern Christian Leadership Conference (SCLC)

Led by the Reverend Ralph Abernathy, a group of poor and militant people, largely black and from the South, gathered in make-shift tents near Washington's Capitol to dramatize their demand for better civil and economic rights. It was a short-lived, but dramatic, "poor people's crusade."

613. U.S.A. Southern Christian Leadership Conference (SCLC).

614. U.S.A. Southern Christian Leadership Conference (SCLC).

Invasion of Czechoslovakia. August, 1968.

615. Czechoslovakia. On sword, "treason."

616. Czechoslovakia. *This is your work.*

617.

618. Czechoslovakia. *USSR: This is the counterrevolution.*

619. Czechoslovakia.

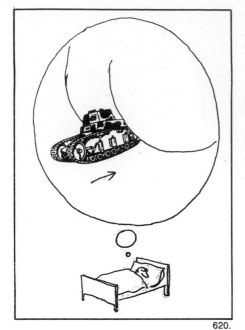

620.   621.   622.

623.   624.   625.

626.   627.

628.

629.

LA DISPERAZIONE REGNA IN CECOSLOVACCHIA

JAN PALACH
CADUTO PER LA LIBERTÀ

CONTRO UN SISTEMA OPPRESSORE DI POPOLI

I democratici cristiani si sentono uniti, nel dolore e nello sdegno, alla disperazione del popolo cecoslovacco.

I giovani di Praga, di Pilsen e di Brno contestano fino all'estremo sacrificio l'occupazione militare sovietica e i compromessi dei loro capi. Essi esigono:

VIA LE TRUPPE SOVIETICHE. PIENA LIBERTA' AI POPOLI E AI CITTADINI!

I comunisti italiani non possono più limitarsi a deplorare, ma devono denunciare apertamente i responsabili della tragica catena di orrendi suicidi. Solo così il loro dolore può trasformarsi in vera solidarietà.

✝ LA DEMOCRAZIA CRISTIANA

D.C.·SPES

630.

631.

620. Czechoslovakia.

621. Czechoslovakia. *We are the boys from "Tass". We inform the masses.*

622. Czechoslovakia.

623. Czechoslovakia.

624. Czechoslovakia. *You too are guilty for occupying Czechoslovakia.*

625. Czechoslovakia. *Go and kill!*

626. U.S.A. Young Americans for Freedom. 1969.

627. Great Britain. Independent Information Centre. 1968.

628, 629. Posters of Dubcek and Svoboda displayed in shop windows and other public places, Prague, September, 1968.

630. Italy. Christian Democratic Party. *Despair reigns in Czechoslovakia. Jan Palach: Fallen in the name of liberty against a system of oppression of the people . . . Away with the Soviet troops. Full liberty to the people and towns!!* 1968.

631. France. Atelier Populaire de Marseille. *Prague 68. Did the Soviet intervention save Socialism from danger? The revolutionary movement must answer this question. It must prevent reactionaries from using it as a weapon against Communism. Let us not confuse Socialism with bureaucracy. Meeting and debate.* 1968.

Mexico Olympics. October, 1968.

632.

633.

634.

Students used the worldwide publicity given the Olympics in Mexico to focus on their grievances against their government. As can be seen from Figure 632, some athletes also joined in.

632. U.S.A. Two black American athletes surprised the audience by giving the black power symbol upon receiving their medals.

633. Mexico. National Strike Committee (CNH). *Student movement. We demand the solution to Mexico's problems.*

634. Mexico. National Strike Committee (CNH). *We won't give in. The fight goes on.*

635. Mexico. *I'm for . . . imperialism and its lackeys.*

636. Mexico. *Away with the Granderos* (special police force).

637. Mexico. *The dialogue must go in public.*

638. Mexico. *We demand the demarcation of responsibilities.* President Díaz Ordaz.

639. Mexico. *Put on your pajamas and jump into bed, because it's sleeping time.*

635.

636.

637.

638.

639.

640. Mexico. *People unite. We will not beg for freedom!*

641. Mexico. *Behind every dead student, there is a mother who demands justice.*

642. Mexico. *Free the political prisoners.*

643. Mexico. *Aggressors against the Mexican people.*

644. Mexico. National Strike Committee (CNH). *We're united: if I go forward, follow me; if I hang back, push me if I betray you, kill me; if I am killed, avenge me. Forward to victory . . . forever!*

645. Mexico. *Hypocritcal and murderous government! Men must die but ideas don't.*

Cambodian Invasion. April, 1970.

646. U.S.A.
647. U.S.A. Student Mobilization Committee. Call for a nationwide strike on May 5.
648. U.S.A. Student Mobilization Committee to End War in Vietnam.
649. France. Faculté de Vincennes. *For Nixon, Indochina is Dienbienphu.*
650. U.S.A. Student Mobilization Committee to End the War in Southeast Asia.

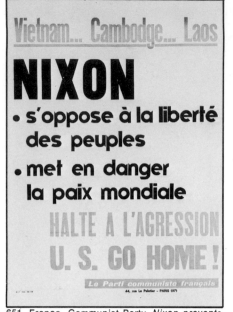

651. France. Communist Party. *Nixon prevents freedom of the people; endangers world peace. Stop the aggression.* 1970.

652. U.S.A. Harvard University Student Strike. 1970.

653. U.S.A. Rhode Island School of Design Student Strike. 1970.

654. U.S.A. Labor-Student Coalition for Peace. 1970.

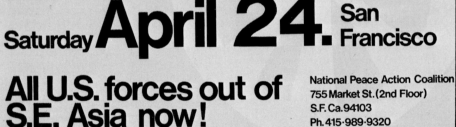

655. U.S.A. National Peace Action Coalition. 1970.

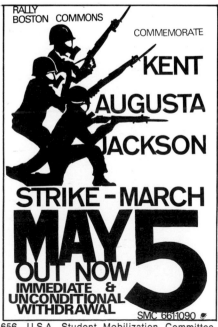

656. U.S.A. Student Mobilization Committee. 1970.

657. U.S.A. 1970.

658. U.S.A. Student Mobilization Committee to End the War in Southeast Asia. 1970.

659. South America. Artist: Giudith Sklar.

660. South America. Artist: Carlos Alonso.

Rockefeller's Visit to South America. May, 1968.

President Nixon appointed New York's governor, Nelson Rockefeller, as his envoy to improve relations in Latin America. Rockefeller received a mixed reaction; students, especially, voiced anti-American sentiments.

661. South America. Out. Artist: Marta Peluffo.

662. South America. Artist: Antoni Berni.

663. South America. *Welcome*. Artist: Mario Mollari.

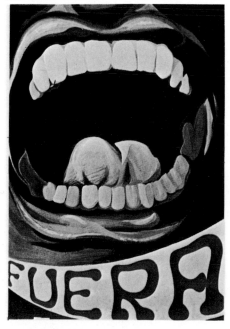

664. Chile. *Chile puts on long pants. Now copper is Chilean!* 1971.

665. Chile. *On the nationalization of copper in 1971, we are present!* 1971.

666. Chile. *Long live Chile. At last copper is ours!* 1971.

667. Cuba. Cuban Committee for South Vietnam. *Why a war in Vietnam? Tenacity, organization, discipline. Daily heroism at work. Ten years of anti-Yankee struggle by the Vietnamese people. Ten million tons of sugar.*

668. Cuba. OSPAAAL. *Nixon.* 1971.

669. Cuba. OSPAAAL. 1970.

670. France. Communist Party. *Withdrawal of American troops, The only solution to Vietnam.* 1970.

This section shows how the poster can be used as a medium of dialogue in communicating pro and con opinions on the burning issues of the day. In addition, Communist Parties drew public notice by massive celebrations of their victories.

COMO EN VIETNAM
TENACIDAD, ORGANIZACION, DISCIPLINA, HEROISMO DIARIO EN EL TRABAJO

"DIEZ AÑOS DE LUCHA ANTIYANQUI DEL PUEBLO VIETNAMITA, DIEZ MILLONES DE TONELADAS DE AZUCAR".

Comité Cubano de Solidaridad con Viet Nam del Sur

667.

Vietnam

668.

Del 13 al 19 de marzo / march 13-19 / du 13 au 19 mars

Todos con Viet Nam
Together with Viet Nam
Tous avec le Viet Nam

669.

RETRAIT DES TROUPES AMERICAINES

seule solution au Vietnam

LE PARTI COMMUNISTE FRANÇAIS

670.

êtes-vous solidaires de ceux qui massacrent au Vietnam?

luttez contre le Pacte Atlantique qui lie la France à l'impérialisme américain

PSU 81 rue Mademoiselle-Paris 15

671.

amerikanen uit vietnam

steun aan het bevrijdingsfront

672.

ICAP

673.

1969

Committee for Cultural Relations with Foreign Countries
HANOI D R VIETNAM

674.

Amerikanen uit Vietnam!

Kom naar het Waarheidfestival, 20 oktober, Nieuwe Rai, Amsterdam.

675.

中国七亿人民是越南人民的坚强后盾
ZHONG GUO QI YI REN MIN SHI YUE NAN REN MIN DE JIAN QIANG HOU DUN

676.

越南人民抗击美国侵略者
展览图片

677.

678.

679.

681.

680.

671. France. Communist Party. *Are you in agreement with those who massacre in Vietnam. Fight against NATO, which ties France to American imperialism.* 1969.

672. Netherlands. Committee to Help the National Liberation Front. *Americans out of Vietnam. Support the National Liberation Front.* 1968.

673. Cuba. Cuban Institute for Friendship with Foreign Peoples (ICAP). 1971.

674. North Vietnam. Committee for Cultural Relations with Foreign Countries. Calendar with picture of militia girl in coastal areas, North Vietnam. 1969.

675. Netherlands. *Americans out of Vietnam!* 1968.

676. China. *The 700,000,000 Chinese people are the firm support of the Vietnamese people.*

677. China. *The Vietnamese people resist the American invader.* Announcement of an exhibition of pictures. 1967.

678. Austria. Communist Party. *This picture shocked the world.* The chief of the South Vietnamese shot a handcuffed victim on the open street in Saigon. Hitler admirer General Ky commented, "Such events are normal." 1968.

679. Cuba. "Planting Rice." Silkscreen. Artist: Rene Mederos.

680. France. Communist Youth Movement. *Youth and students: Let us collect to equip 1000 young Vietnamese. Let us assure the success of May 10,* 1970.

681. Cuba. "Guerilla Fighter." Silkscreen. Artist: Rene Mederos. 1970.

682. Cuba. *For the 10-point plan: Withdrawal, self-determination, and reunification.* 1969.

683.

684.

1969

685.

686.

683. China. "The righteous patriotic struggle of the Vietnamese people in opposing the American-Diem block will win the great victory in all spheres not only political but military as well. We the Chinese people resolutely support the South Vietnamese people's righteous struggle."—Mao Tse-tung.

684. China. What is the real steel wall? It is the masses. They are the millions who genuinely support revolution. This is the real wall of steel. No force can break it.

685. North Vietnam. Committee for Cultural Relations with Foreign Countries. Calendar with picture of girl guerilla at Cu Chi, South Vietnam. 1969.

686. Cuba. OSPAAAL. 1970.

687. U.S.A. United Women's Contingent. 1971.

688. U.S.A. Student Mobilization Committee to End War in Vietnam. Photographer: Richard Avedon. Designer: Marvin Israel. 1969.

Vietnam CONTINUED

689. U.S.A. Student Mobilization Committee to End the War in Vietnam. 1969.

690. U.S.A. Advertisement for film.

691. U.S.A. The New Mobilization Committee. 1969.

692. U.S.A. Artist: J. Refregier. 1970.

Vietnam CONTINUED

BRING THE GIs HOME NOW

VOTE SOCIALIST WORKERS IN 68

FRED HALSTEAD FOR PRESIDENT
PAUL BOUTELLE FOR VICE PRESIDENT

YOUNG SOCIALISTS FOR HALSTEAD AND BOUTELLE 873 Broadway New York N.Y. 10003

693. U.S.A. Socialist Workers Party. 1968.

694. U.S.A. Student Mobilization Committee (SMC) 1970.

695. U.S.A. People's Coalition for Peace and Justice. Based on a drawing of Ben Shahn. 1971.

696. U.S.A. Young Americans for Freedom. 1969.

They've got an invisible program to end an undeclared war backed by a silent majority.

Madison Square Garden Rally: 1970 Senators for Peace and New Priorities.
Thursday, March 12, 7:30 P.M.

704.

Two more casualties of Viet Nam.

Is it worth it?

705.

Unfortunately, this is the only deadline we have in Vietnam.

One more death is one too many. Write your Congressman.

706.

704-709. U.S.A. Sponsored by the Committee to Help Unsell The War; a group formed by 35 advertising agencies, 1971.

They're eating us out of house, home, city, school, medical care and clean air.

They're President Thieu and Vice President Ky, the military rulers of South Vietnam.

Help unsell the war.

707.

I AM AGAINST...

708.

The only time we're in the front is when it's time to die.

Stop the war. It's killing us.

709.

END CAMPUS COMPLICITY WITH THE WAR

STUDENT MOBILIZATION COMMITTEE
TO END THE WAR IN VIETNAM

710.

killing to
end war
is like
balling to
end love

711.

UNITE

AGAINST THE WAR

712.

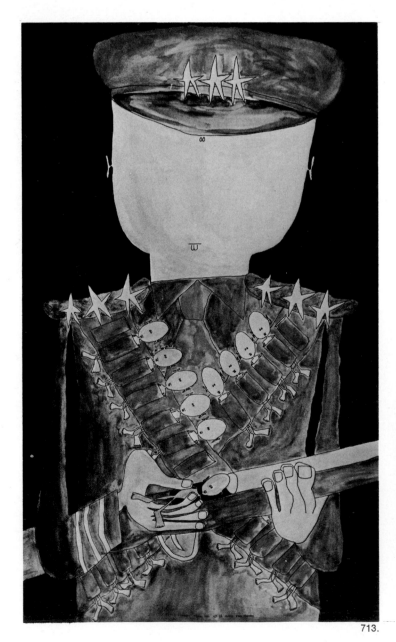

713.

MORATORIUM

714.

Set the date: 1971

715.

716.

717.

718.

Vietnam CONTINUED

710. U.S.A. Student Mobilization Committee to End the War in Vietnam. 1968.
711. U.S.A. Gemini Productions. 1971.
712. U.S.A. 1970.
713. U.S.A. Yippie, Inc. 1971.
714. U.S.A. Artist: Jasper Johns. 1969.
715. U.S.A. 1971.
716. U.S.A. 1970.
717. U.S.A. Student Mobilization Committee. 1968.
718. U.S.A. Young Americans for Freedom. 1969.
719. U.S.A. *Q: And babies? A: And babies.* 1970.
720. U.S.A. Clergy and Laymen Concerned About Vietnam and Fellowship of Reconciliation. National Lenten Passover Fast Action Project. February-April, 1970.

719.

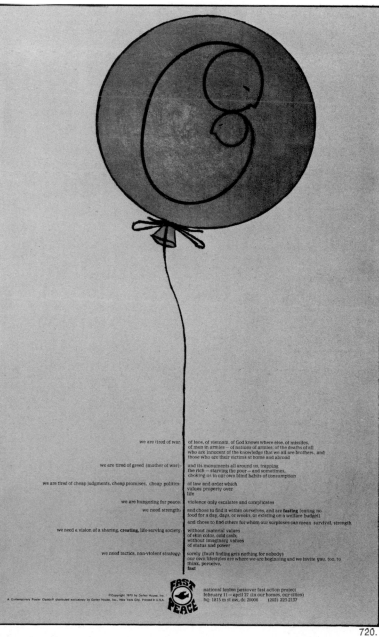

720.

BE COUNTED THIS TIME
MARCH TO END THE WAR
WASHINGTON, APRIL 24

Join your neighbors. Come to Washington, Saturday, April 24th.

Buses from: **Mt. Kisco** **New Rochelle** **White Plains**
RR Station Quaker Ridge County Center
Shopping Center

For reservations: **Write** Westchester Peace Council, Box 5H Scarsdale, N.Y. 10583
Phone 723-7808 $12.00 round trip

721.

ENOUGH!
OUT NOW

APRIL 24
NPAC

722.

STOP WAR

723.

Whose side are you on

theirs or Nixon's?

BRING ALL THE GIs HOME NOW!
END THE DRAFT NOW!

MARCH ON WASHINGTON
APRIL 24

724.

HELP PLAN
THE FALL ANTIWAR ACTIONS
END THE DRAFT
BRING ALL THE TROOPS
HOME NOW

NATIONAL ANTIWAR CONVENTION
JULY 2, 3, & 4, 1971
HUNTER COLLEGE, 68TH & PARK AVE.
RALLY FRIDAY, JULY 2 7:30 P.M.
ADMISSION $1.50

725.

G.E. OFF CAMPUS!
GE

AND GE PRODUCTS
TOO!

war profit
is their most
important product.

BRING ALL THE G.I.'S HOME, NOW!

s.m.c STUDENT MOBILIZATION COMMITTEE TO END THE WAR IN VIETNAM
1029 VERMONT AVE N.W. WASHINGTON DC. 20005 TEL. 202 - 737 - 0072

726.

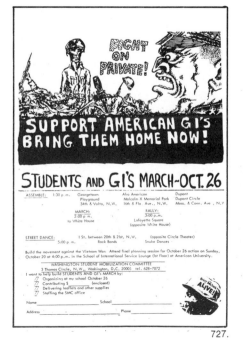

FIGHT ON PRIVATE!

SUPPORT AMERICAN GI'S
BRING THEM HOME NOW!

STUDENTS AND GI'S MARCH—OCT. 26

ASSEMBLE: 1:30 p.m. Georgetown Afro American Dupont
Playground Malcolm X Memorial Park Dupont Circle
34th & Volta, N.W. 16th & Fla. Ave., N.W. Mass. & Conn. Ave., N.Y

MARCH: RALLY: 3:00 p.m.
2:00 p.m. Lafayette Square
to White House (opposite White House)

STREET DANCE: 1 St. between 20th & 21st, N.W. (opposite Circle Theater)
5:00 p.m. Rock Bands Snake Dances

Build the movement against the Vietnam War. Attend final planning session for October 26 action on Sunday,
October 20 at 4:00 p.m., in the School of International Service Lounge (lst floor) at American University.

WASHINGTON STUDENT MOBILIZATION COMMITTEE
3 Thomas Circle, N.W., Washington, D.C., 20005 rel. 628-7072
I want to help build STUDENTS AND GI'S MARCH by:
☐ Organizing at my school October 26
☐ Contributing $ (enclosed)
☐ Delivering leaflets and other supplies
☐ Staffing the SMC office

Name _____ School _____
Address _____ Phone _____

727.

You may fool all the
people some of the time;
you can even fool some
of the people all the time;

BUT YOU CAN'T FOOL ALL
OF THE PEOPLE ALL THE TIME.

DEMONSTRATE
APRIL 24

Bring all the GI's home—End the draft NOW!
March on Washington & San Francisco

728.

. . . the U.S. Government
continues, methodically,
to murder thousands of
innocent Vietnamese . . .
how much longer can the
American people accept
this horror? . . .

WED. APRIL 15 11:30 A.M.
Spring Offensive To End
The War On Vietnam

INTERNAL REVENUE SERVICE
HEADQUARTERS
Church & Murray Streets Manhattan

THE PEOPLE ARE
GETTING TOGETHER!

VIETNAM LAOS CAMBODIA
ALL U.S. FORCES OUT NOW!

729.

730.

731.

Vietnam CONTINUED

721. U.S.A. Westchester Peace Council. 1971.
722. U.S.A. National Peace Action Coalition (NPAC). 1971.
723. U.S.A. Cocorico Graphics. 1970.
724. U.S.A. National Peace Action Coalition. 1971.
725. U.S.A. National Peace Action Coalition. 1971.
726. U.S.A. Student Mobilization Committee to End the War in Vietnam. 1969.
727. U.S.A. Washington Student Mobilization Committee. Leaflet.
728. U.S.A. National Peace Action Coalition. 1971.
729. U.S.A. Vietnam Peace Parade Committee. 1970.
730. U.S.A. *Scapegoat*. Lieutenant Calley, convicted of murdering civilians at My Lai, South Vietnam. 1971.
731. U.S.A. Artist: Mark Podwal. 1969.
732. U.S.A. 1970.

732.

THEY'RE THE REASON
WE'RE IN VIETNAM

733.

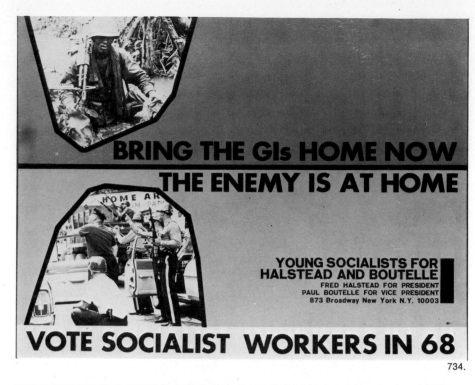

BRING THE GIs HOME NOW
THE ENEMY IS AT HOME

YOUNG SOCIALISTS FOR
HALSTEAD AND BOUTELLE
FRED HALSTEAD FOR PRESIDENT
PAUL BOUTELLE FOR VICE PRESIDENT
873 Broadway New York N.Y. 10003

VOTE SOCIALIST WORKERS IN 68

734.

HELP END
DEMONSTRATIONS

NO
VIET CONG
EVER CALLED
ME NIGGER

STOP
THE
WAR

735.

ORDERS
FROM: NGUYEN HUU THO
PRESIDENT OF THE PRESIDIUM OF THE COMMUNIST NATIONAL
LIBERATION FRONT IN SOUTH VIET NAM - 28 OCTOBER 1969

TO: AMERICANS PARTICIPATING IN THE FALL
OFFENSIVE AT HOME.

YOU WILL...
EXTEND YOUR POSITIVE PARTICIPATION IN
THE CONTINUING STRUGGLE ON NOVEMBER
15TH AND IN THE FOLLOWING MONTHS;

COMPEL THE NIXON ADMINISTRATION TO
REPATRIATE THE U.S. EXPEDITIONARY
CORPS.

WHOSE SIDE
ARE YOU ON ?

HAWAII FOUNDATION FOR AMERICAN FREEDOMS

736.

the fight for freedom...

is at home!

STRIKE! NOV 14
MARCH ON WASHINGTON
& SAN FRANCISCO NOV 15

BRING ALL THE GIS HOME NOW!

737.

Vietnam CONTINUED

733. U.S.A. National Student Committee for Victory in Vietnam.
734. U.S.A. Socialist Workers Party. 1968.
U.S.A. 1970.
736. U.S.A. Hawaii Foundation for American Freedoms. 1969.
737. U.S.A. Student Mobilization Committee to End the War in Vietnam. 1970.
738. U.S.A. National Peace Action Coalition. 1971.
739. U.S.A. G.I. Civil Liberties Defense Committee. 1971.
740. U.S.A. National Peace Action Coalition. 1971.
741. U.S.A. Protesting closing of Ft. Dix coffee house, May 16, 1970.
742. U.S.A. National Peace Action Coalition. 1971.

STOP THEM!
they can't stop themselves

MARCH ON WASHINGTON—SAN FRANCISCO **APRIL 24, 1971**

NATIONAL PEACE ACTION COALITION

738.

GIs United
Against the War.
Ft. Jackson.

Fighting men.

739.

MARCH FOR PEACE APRIL 24

CONSTRUCTION YES—DESTRUCTION NO!

THE VIETNAMESE NEVER FROZE MY WAGES

GET OUT NOW!

LABOR CONTINGENT ASSEMBLE AT 10:00 A.M., KIMBELL PARK, GEARY AND STEINER STREETS
MARCH TO RALLY 1:30 P.M., POLO FIELD, GOLDEN GATE PARK
ENDORSED BY SAN FRANCISCO, SANTA CLARA, CONTRA COSTA AND SAN MATEO LABOR COUNCILS, AFL-CIO
NATIONAL PEACE ACTION COALITION, Labor Support Committee, 755 Market Street, San Francisco · Phone 989-9320

740.

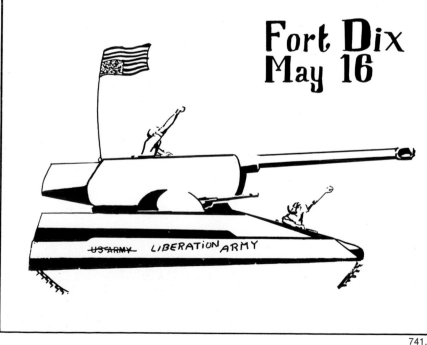

Fort Dix
May 16

741.

742.

Liberation

743.

744.

745.

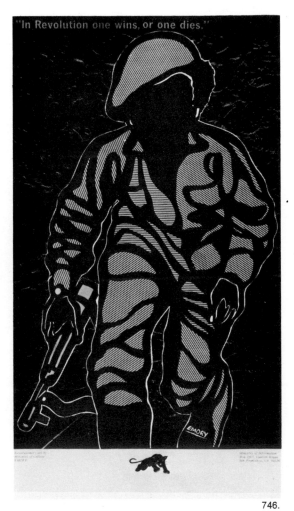

746.

747.

749.

750.

748.

BLACKS

743. U.S.A. National Urban Coalition. 1971.
744. U.S.A. "Black Uncle Sam." 1968.
745. U.S.A. Black Panther Party. 1970.
746. U.S.A. Black Panther Party. 1970
747. U.S.A. Student Nonviolent Coordinating Committee (SNCC). Malcolm X. Photo: Francis Mitchele.
748. U.S.A. Black Panther Party. 1970.
749. U.S.A. "Chicago 7."
750. U.S.A. Malcolm X.
751. U.S.A. Black Panther Party. Fred Hampton, 1969.

751.

BLACK IS BETTER
THAN ANOTHER HUE,
IN THAT IT SCORNS
TO BEAR ANOTHER HUE.
William Shakespeare
TITUS ANDRONICUS

752.

753.

754.

BLACKS CONTINUED

752. U.S.A.
753. U.S.A. "Black is better."
754. U.S.A. Ku Klux Klan (KKK). 1969.
755. U.S.A. Black Panther Party. 1970.
756. U.S.A. Statecraft. 1969.
757. U.S.A. Phoenix House, 1970.

755.

756.

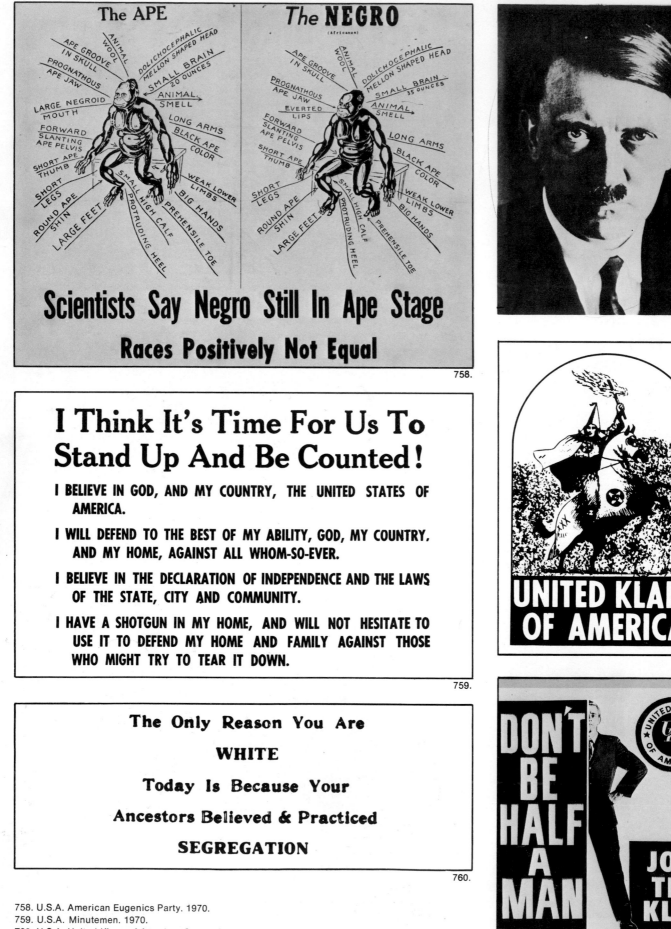

758. U.S.A. American Eugenics Party. 1970.
759. U.S.A. Minutemen. 1970.
760. U.S.A. United Klans of America. Card. 1970.
761. U.S.A. National Socialist White People's Party. Adolf Hitler. Photograph distributed to members. 1969.
762. U.S.A. United Klans of America. 1969.
763. U.S.A. United Klans of America. 1970.

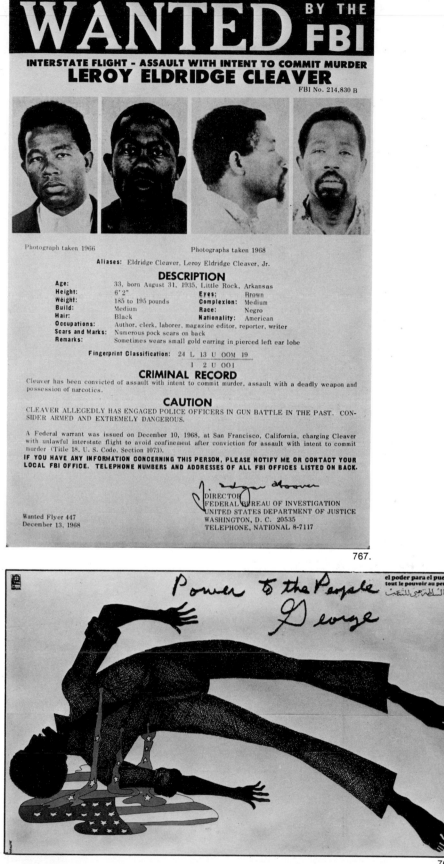

764. Cuba. OSPAAAL. 1968.

765. China. *We firmly support the American Negroes in their struggle. The evil imperialist system rose with the slave trade, and it will be defeated when the black people are liberated.* 1967.

766. Cuba. "Disappearance of Ben Barka" (Moroccan leader, presumed murdered, whose assassin has never been found).

767. U.S.A. F.B.I. "Most Wanted" Flyer, printed and distributed commercially.

768. Cuba. OSPAAAL. *"Power to the People"* — George Jackson, a "Soledad brother," imprisoned on a charge of burglary and subsequently killed. 1971.

769.

770.

771.

772.

773.

774.

775.

776.

777.

Liberation

BLACKS AND PUERTO RICANS

769. U.S.A. Young Lords Party (made up of Puerto Ricans living in New York City). Cover of *Palante*, Young Lords' newspaper. 1971.

770. U.S.A. Young Lords Party. 1970.

771. U.S.A. Young Lords Party. *Julio Roldan, assassinated by the police.* 1970.

772. U.S.A. Young Lords Party. 1971.

773. U.S.A. Young Lords Party. *We want self-determination for all Latin brothers and sisters. Solidarity with Latin America.*

774. U.S.A. Young Lords Party. 1971.

775. U.S.A. Socialist Workers Campaign Committee. 1968.

776. China. 1967.

777. U.S.A. Juan Farinas Defense Committee. 1970.

778. U.S.A. *Long live free Puerto Rico!* 1969.

778.

Liberation CONTINUED

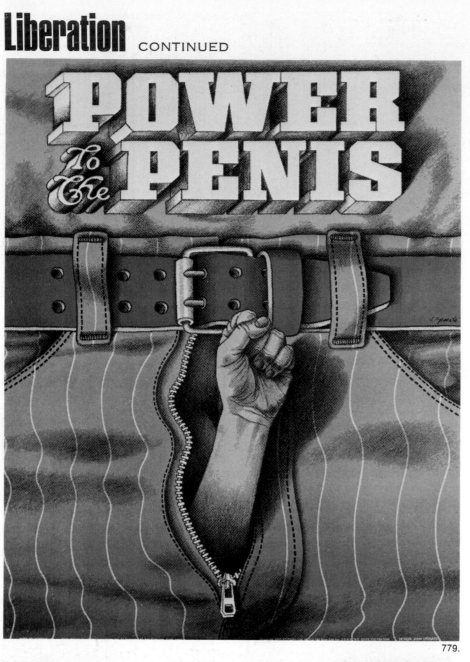

779.

780.

781.

782.

783.

WOMEN

779. U.S.A. Design: John Sposato. 1970.
780. U.S.A. Photographed by Elizabeth Richter.
781. U.S.A. Women's Strike Coalition. 1971.
782. U.S.A. Congress to Unite Women. 1970.
783. U.S.A.
784. U.S.A. Artist: Guillermo.
785. U.S.A.
786. U.S.A.
787. U.S.A. Women register to vote in the 1920's.
788. U. S. A. Black Panther Party. 1970.

784.

785.

786.

787.

788.

789.

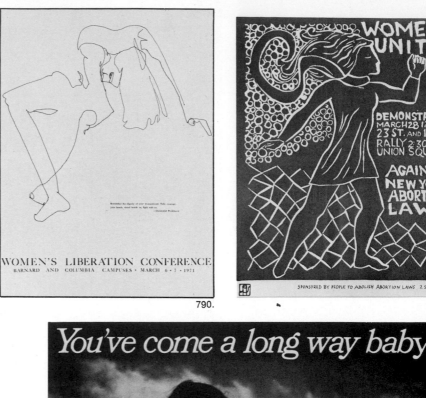

790.

791.

792.

794.

793.

Liberation / **WOMEN** CONTINUED

795.

796.

ROSA LUXEMBURG 1919-1969

'Where the chains of capitalism are forged, there must the chains be broken. That only is socialism and thus only can socialism be brought into being.'

797.

Would you be more careful if it was you who got pregnant?

798.

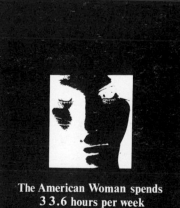

The American Woman spends
3 3.6 hours per week
in personal grooming;
9 9.6 hours per week
performing household duties.

you've only got one life to live.

Women's liberation.

36 west 22 st. nyc, ny, tel. 961 1860

799.

789. U.S.A.
790. U.S.A. 1971.
791. U.S.A. People to Abolish Abortion. 1970.
792. U.S.A. Women's Strike for Equality. 1971.
793. U.S.A.
794. U.S.A. Wespac Communications. 1970.
795. U.S.A. Black Panther Party. 1970.
796. U.S.A. 1971.
797. U.S.A. A tribute to early socialist leader for women's rights. 1969.
798. U.S.A.
799. U.S.A.

800. North Vietnam. *"With best wishes for American Women's Liberation."* 1970.

801. East Germany. *60th anniversary of International Woman's Day. "Fight where life is."—Clara Zetkin.* 1970.

802. France. Communist Party. *The woman today . . . tomorrow.* Announcement of meeting. 1970.

803. Canada. Abortion Campaign Committee. 1971.

804. U.S.A. (Printed on silver mylar) 1971.

805. U.S.A. Socialist Workers Campaign Committee. 1970.

806. U.S.A. Arthur Rice. 1970.

807.

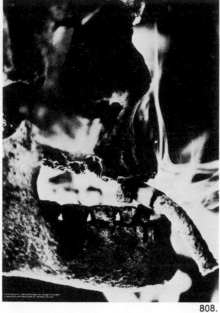

808.

809.

810.

811.

812.

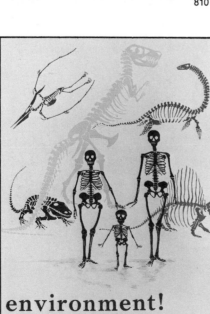

813.

814.

Ecology

807. U.S.A. 1970.
808. U.S.A. 1971.
809. U.S.A. 1971.
810. U.S.A.
811. U.S.A. Advertisement. 1971.
812. U.S.A. 1969.
813. U.S.A. Environment! 1970.
814. U.S.A. 1970.

815.

816.

817.

818.

819.

820.

815. U.S.A. Designer: Michaele Heinichen.
1970.
816.–818. U.S.A. Environmental Action Coalition.
1970.
817. U.S.A. 1971.
819. U.S.A. 1971.
820. U.S.A. 1970.
821. U.S.A. Reference to oil slick off coast
of Santa Barbara, Calif., that killed many
birds. Photo: Benhari. 1970.

821.

822. U.S.A. 1970

Father forgive them for they know not what they do.

823. U.S.A. 1970.

824.

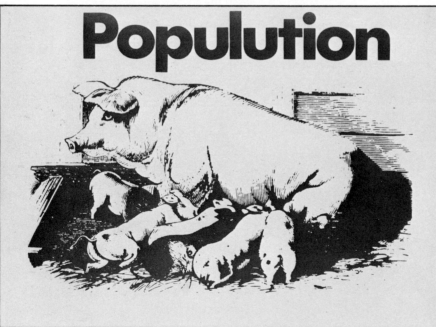

825.

Caution:
Keep out
of reach of
children*

827.

824. U.S.A. 1970.

825. U.S.A. 1971.

826. U.S.A. 1970.

827. U.S.A. The Ecology Center. *Milk in such containers may be unfit for human consumption. DDT content 0.10 to 0.30 parts/million in milk of nursing mothers (2 to 6 times the amount allowed in milk for commercial sale).* 1970.

828. U.S.A. Environment Mobilization. 1970.

829. U.S.A. Environment! 1970.

830. U.S.A. 1970:

831. U.S.A. Environment! 1970.

832. U.S.A. Environmental Defense Fund. 1970.

833. U.S.A. 1970.

828.

ENVIRONMENT!

829.

i
sent
a
bird
into
the
air...
he
didn't
find
any,

anywhere

830.

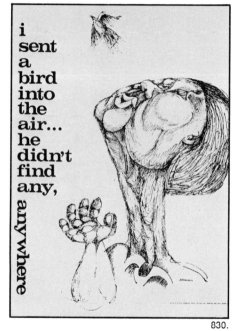

ENVIRONMENT!

179 Fifth Avenue   New York City 10003.   675-8740.

831.

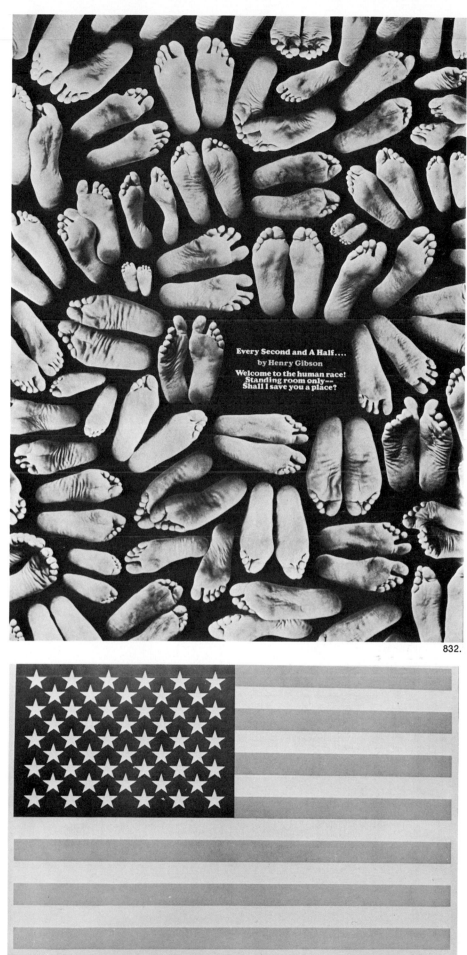

Every Second and A Half....
by Henry Gibson
Welcome to the human race!
Standing room only—
Shall I save you a place?

832.

ECOLOGY NOW!

833.

835. U.S.A. "Save us from Ourselves" series.

The squeeze is on

834. U.S.A. 1971.

836. U.S.A. Artist: Robert Rauschenberg. 1970.

837. U.S.A. Socialist Workers Party. 1970.

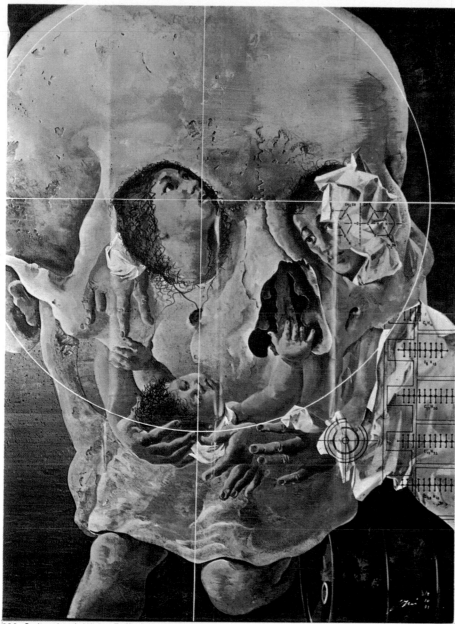

838. Switzerland. Water Pollution poster by Hans Erni. 1971.

840. U.S.A. 1970.

841. U.S.A. Environmental Defense Fund. 1970.

839. U.S.A. 1970.

842. U.S.A. Environmental Action Coalition. 1970.

Communist Celebrations

843.

844.

845.

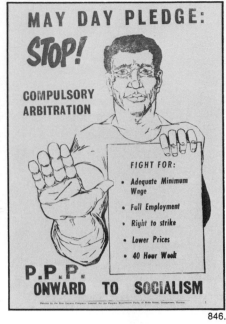

846.

847.

848.

850.

843. U.S.S.R. *Proletariat of all countries unite.* 1967.

844. U.S.S.R. *The glory of these days shall not be forgotten.* 1967.

845. U.S.S.R. *We will never be forgotten because, eternally controlling the weather of the planet, we are really "man."*

846. New Guyana. People's Progressive Party (PPP). *May Day pledge: Stop! Compulsory arbitration.* 1969.

847. East Germany. *The bear is happy. So is the Republic. 15 years of the DDR.*

848. U.S.S.R. *The glory of these days shall not be forgotten.* 1967.

849. U.S.S.R. *Always alert, the invincible Soviet navy. 1968.* 1968.

850. U.S.S.R. *The spark shall kindle the flame.* 1968.

851.

852.

853.

854.

855.

856.

857.

851. U.S.S.R. *Labor shall rule the world.* 1968.
852. U.S.S.R. *To the hero-city of Leningrad.* 1968.
853. U.S.S.R. *We build Communism.* 1968.
854. U.S.S.R. *The ideas of Communism are all-powerful.* 1970.
855. China. Karl Marx. 1970.
856. China. Stalin. 1969.
857. China. Engels. 1969.
858. China. Lenin. 1969.
859. Austria. 1967.
860. Cuba. 1970.

858.

50 JAHRE **REPUBLIK ÖSTERREICH KOMMUNISTISCHE PARTEI** fest

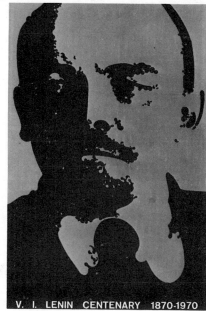

V. I. LENIN CENTENARY 1870-1970

859.

860.

ПЯТИЛЕТКУ-
НА ОТЛИЧНО!

861.

212

nario

МЫ ПАРТИЯ
БУДУЩЕГО,
А БУДУЩЕЕ
ПРИНАДЛЕЖИТ
МОЛОДЕЖИ.
Ленин

Будущее
принадлежит
коммунизму

861. U.S.S.R. *Hero of socialist competition. Let the five-year plan be outstanding.* 1968.

862. Cuba. *Centennial.* 1971.

863. Rumania. *23 August 1925. The Year of the liberation of the fatherland.* 1969.

864. U.S.S.R. *"We, the better party members, belong to the young".* —Lenin. 1970.

865. U.S.S.R. *It's better to belong to Communism.* 1970.

863.

864.

865.

if anyone in days to come should say that we were civilized in this country, this war will be cited as proof we were barbarians.

880.

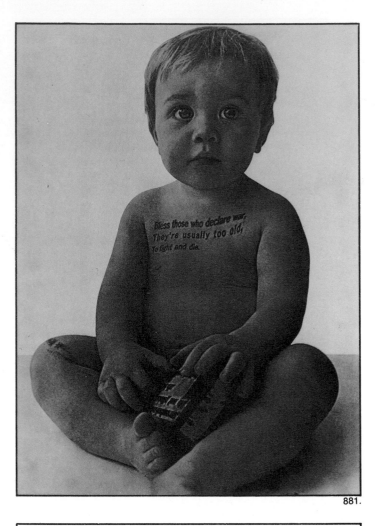

Bless those who declare war. They're usually too old, To fight and die.

881.

war is not healthy for children and other living things

882.

NOTICE

OFFICE OF CIVILIAN DEFENSE
WASHINGTON D. C.

INSTRUCTION TO PATRONS ON PREMISES
IN CASE OF NUCLEAR BOMB ATTACK:

UPON THE FIRST WARNING:

1. STAY CLEAR OF ALL WINDOWS.

2. KEEP HANDS FREE OF GLASSES, BOTTLES, CIGARETTES, ETC.

3. STAND AWAY FROM BAR, TABLES, ORCHESTRA, EQUIPMENT AND FURNITURE.

4. LOOSEN NECKTIE, UNBUTTON COAT AND ANY OTHER RESTRICTIVE CLOTHING.

5. REMOVE GLASSES, EMPTY POCKETS OF ALL SHARP OBJECTS SUCH AS PENS, PENCILS, ETC.

6. IMMEDIATELY UPON SEEING THE BRILLIANT FLASH OF NUCLEAR EXPLOSION, BEND OVER AND PLACE YOUR HEAD FIRMLY BETWEEN YOUR LEGS.

7. THEN KISS YOUR ASS GOODBYE.

883.

884.

885.

886.

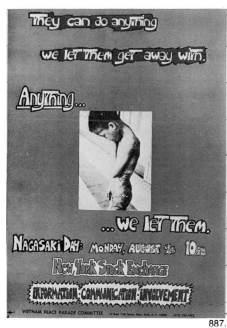

887.

888.

889.

880. U.S.A. Artist: Mark Podwal.
881. U.S.A.
882. U.S.A.
883. U.S.A.
884. U.S.A. President Nixon, Charles Manson and Lt. Calley. 1971.
885. U.S.A. 1971.
886. U.S.A. 1970.
887. U.S.A. Vietnam Peace Parade Committee. 1971.
888. U.S.A. 1970.
889. U.S.A. 1970.
890. U.S.A.
891. U.S.A.

890.

891.

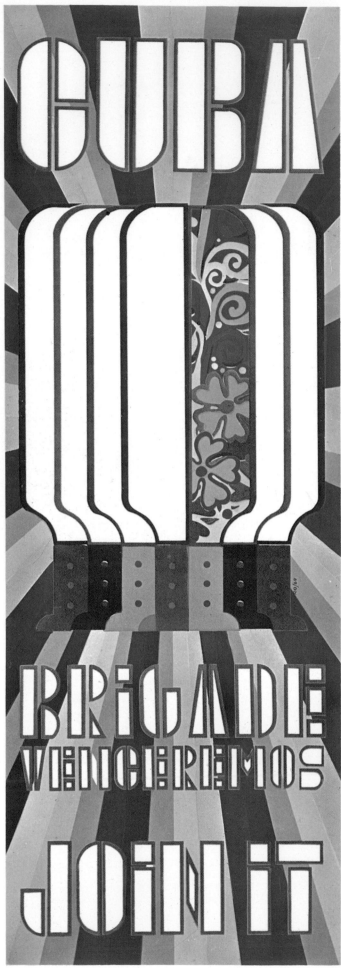

892.

893.

894.

895.

896.

897.

898.

899.

900.

901.

892. Cuba. The Venceremos Brigade is the name of the young Americans who sympathized with Castro's Cuba and went to work in the sugar fields there in the late 1960's. 1969.

893. Cuba. *1959: Liberation. 10th anniversary of the triumph of the revolution.* 1969.

894. Cuba. *1960: Nationalization. 10th anniversary of the triumph of the revolution.* 1969.

895. Cuba. *Victory of Giron (Bay of Pigs). 10th anniversary of the triumph of the revolution.*

896. Cuba. *1962: Crisis of October. 10th anniversary of the triumph of the revolution.* 1969.

897. Cuba. *1963: SMO. 10th anniversary of the triumph of the revolution.*

898. *1964: Voluntary Work. 10th anniversary of the triumph of the revolution.*

899. Cuba. *1965: Central Committee of PCC. 10th anniversary.*

900. Cuba. *1966: Solidarity. 10th anniversary of the triumph of the revolution.* 1969.

901. Cuba. *1968 Offensive. 10th anniversary of the triumph of the revolution.*

902.

Cuba

1968

July 26 — Juillet 26 — Julio 26

CUBA

يومية التضامن مع كوبا ٢٦ تموز ١٩٦٨

OSPAAAL

903.

AL ASALTO DEL MONCADA
DE LOS 10 MILLONES
XVI ANIVERSARIO DEL 26 DE JULIO

26

904.

902. Cuba. *Long live the 26. 10th anniversary of the triumph of the revolution.* 1969.

903. Cuba. *July 26, 1968.* Castro's original activity was called the "26th of July" movement. 1968.

904. Cuba. *Attack the harvesting of the 10 million tons of sugar — the assault on the Moncada.* 1970.

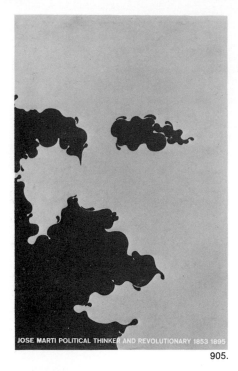

905.

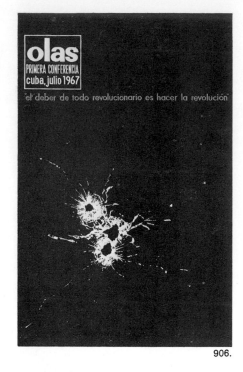

906.

907.

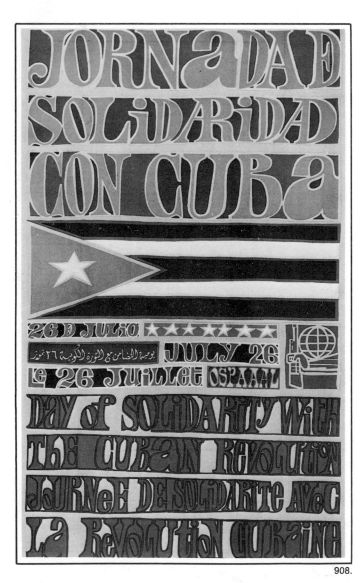

908.

909.

905. Cuba. Institute for Relations with Foreign Peoples (ICAP). 1971.
906. Cuba. *The task of every revolutionary is to make revolution.*
907. Cuba. Institute for Relations with Foreign Peoples (ICAP).
908. Cuba. OSPAAAL. *Day of Solidarity with Cuba.* 1970.
909. Cuba. Committee for the defense of the Revolution (CDR). *In any street, in any block, be on guard always (against counter-revolution). 28th of September, the 9th anniversary of CDR.* 1969.

910.

911.

OTHER HANDS WILL TAKE UP THE WEAPONS.

912.

913.

914.

910. *Cuba: 10th anniversary of revolution. Ever onward to victory. Che Guevara.* 1969.

911. Cuba. Committee for the defense of the Revolution (CDR). *We will achieve the CDR. The 10 million tons of sugar are on the way.* 1970.

912. Cuba. Institute for Relations with Foreign Peoples (ICAP). 1971.

913. U.S.A. Young Socialist Alliance. *Hail Cuba, liberated land of America.* 1968.

914. Cuba. *The aim of Communism is not to create a conscience with money but richness of conscience.* 1968.

915.

916.

LA JUVENTUD A LA VANGUARDIA

917.

Cuba CONTINUED

915. Cuba. 1968.
916. Cuba. *16th anniversary: With the same determination, the same decisiveness, the same discipline as the heroes of Moncada.* 1969.
917. Cuba. *Youth in the vanguard.*

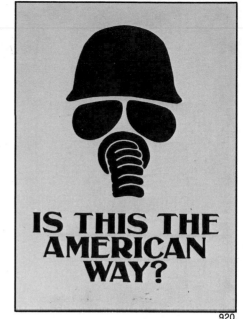

IS THIS THE AMERICAN WAY?

918.

919.

920.

Come together. Independence Day, July 4th, 1970. Wash, DC

921.

Anti-Establishment

918. U.S.A. 1967.
919. U.S.A. *"We are one: Woodstock."* 1969.
920. U.S.A. 1970.
921. U.S.A. Right a Wrong (RAW). For the legalization of marijuana. 1970.
922. U.S.A. 1970.
923. U.S.A. 1970.
924. U.S.A. 1970.

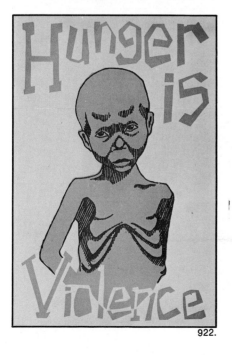

Hunger is Violence

HE DIDN'T PROTEST EITHER

922.

923.

924.

925.

925. U.S.A. George Wallace, governor of Alabama, often considered pro-segre-gationist, with Shirley Chisholm, Democratic Congresswoman from New York City. Artist: Alfred Gescheidt. 1971.

926. U.S.A. Protesting the draft. 1971.

927. U.S.A. *"The whole world is watching.* 1968.

928. U.S.A. 1970.

929. U.S.A. Youth International Party. 1970.

927.

AMERICA

928.

DO iT!

929.

930.

931.

933.

930. U.S.A. 1970.
931. U.S.A. Student at Columbia University, New York City, alleged victim of "police brutality" when police were ordered to clear out the university buildings that students had occupied for three days.
932. U.S.A. 1970.
933. U.S.A. "The Coalition." 1970.
934. U.S.A. "In God We Trust." 1971.

932.

934.

935.

936.

937.

938.

935. U.S.A. Young Americans for Freedom. 1969.
936. U.S.A. Artist: Lou Myers. 1970.
937. U.S.A. A reference to *Fortune* Magazine, which covers business and finance. 1968.
938. U.S.A. Young Americans for Freedom. 1969.
939. U.S.A. United Book Guild.
940. U.S.A. "Protest." 1970.
941. U.S.A. Photo: Lawrence Cameron. 1971.
942. U.S.A. Picture of a hippie. 1969.
943. U.S.A. Artist: Michael Lynne. 1969.
944. U.S.A. Photo Bill Stetner. 1970.

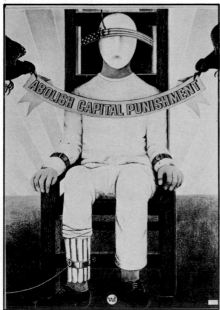

939.

940.

941.

942.

943.

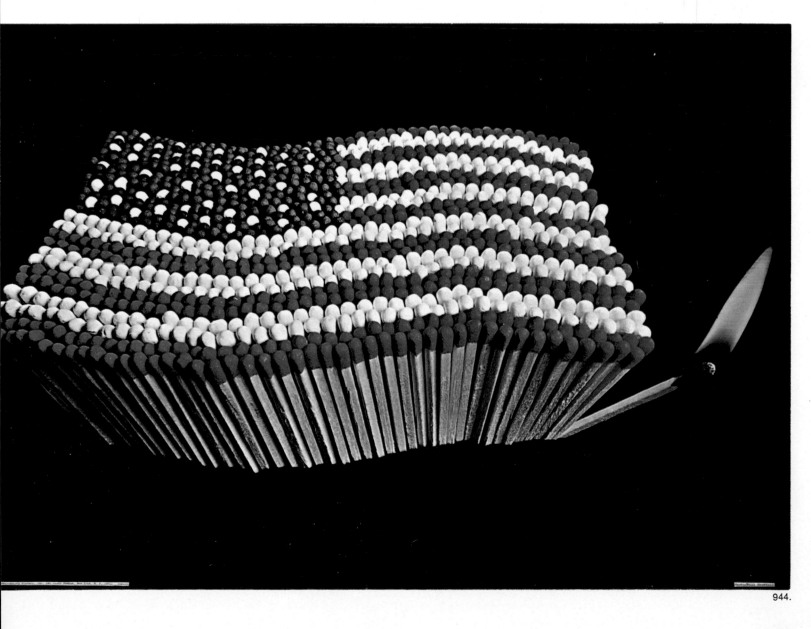

944.

945. U.S.A. Protesting corruption of American life. 1970.

946. U.S.A. 1969.

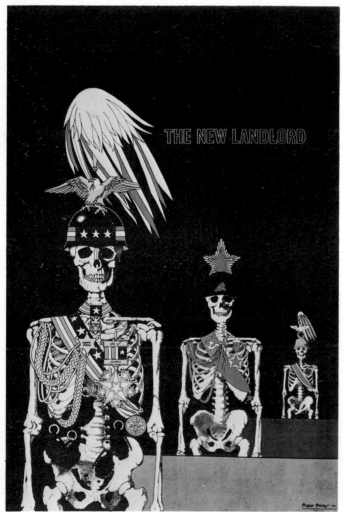

947. U.S.A. Artist: Marshall Baer. 1971.

948. U.S.A. "Superman." 1971.

949. U.S.A. "Face of America." 1970.

950. U.S.A. Mothers' Crusade for Victory over Communism.

952. U.S.A. "Our Gang." (Brandt, De Gaulle, Pope Paul, Moshe Dayan, Nasser, U Thant, Nixon, Castro, Mao Tse-tung). 1969.

951. U.S.A.

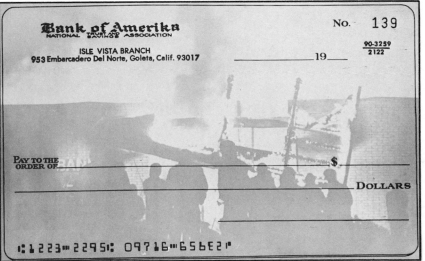
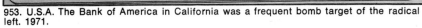

953. U.S.A. The Bank of America in California was a frequent bomb target of the radical left. 1971.

954.

955.

956.

954. Great Britain. Issued by The Great American Disaster Restaurant, London. 1970.

955. U.S.A. 1970.

956. Cuba. *Giron (Bay of Pigs): First defeat of Yankee imperialism in America, 1969: The year of the decisive effort.* 1969.

957. U.S.A. The Patriotic Party. The gun lobby is considered a right-wing group. 1969.

958. U.S.A. 1968.

959. U.S.A. Hawaii Foundation for American Freedoms, Inc. 1969.

960. U.S.A. 1970.

957.

958.

959.

960.

The Army

961. U.S.A. 1971.

963. U.S.A.

962. U.S.A. The issue of hiring veterans became especially acute as the U. S. withdrew from Vietnam, which coincided with a serious unemployment problem. 1971.

964. U.S.A. Pandora Productions, Inc. 1969.

965. U.S.A. Gross National Product Company. 1968.

Join the Army; travel to exotic, distant lands; meet exciting, unusual people and kill them.

Rosner

966.

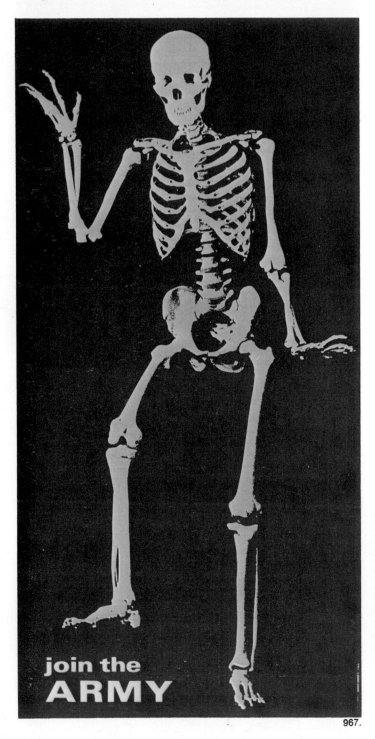

join the ARMY

967.

966. U.S.A. 1971.
967. Denmark.
968. U.S.A. *Old Soldiers Never Die, Young Ones Do.*
969. U.S.A. U.S. Marine Corps. 1971.
970. U.S.A. Artist: William Gibbs, 1971.
971. U.S.S.R. *The undying great heroic deeds of the people.* 1967.
972. Netherlands. 1971.

968.

969.

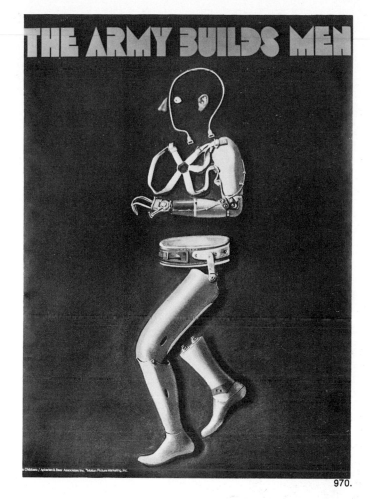

970.

971.

972.

235

NIXON LO VUOLE

SOTTO IL SEGNO
DELLA NATO

aggressione
guerra
fascismo
colonialismo

973.

974.

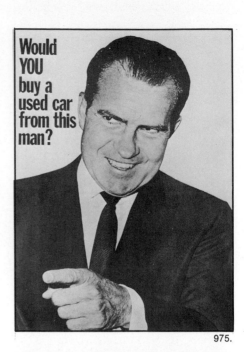

Would YOU buy a used car from this man?

975.

Nixon

973. Italy. Nixon wants it. *Under the symbol of NATO, we have aggression, fascism, colonialism.*

974. U.S.A. 1971.

975. U.S.A. 1968.

976. U.S.A. New Right Coalition (NRC). 1971.

977. U.S.A. 1968.

978. U.S.A. 1970.

979. U.S.A. Artist: Bob Dara. 1970.

980. U.S.A. Americans for Democratic Action (ADA). 1971.

981. U.S.A. "King Richard." Artist: Robert Short. 1970.

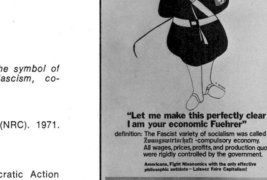

Nixonomics-Phase 3?

"Let me make this perfectly clear
I am your economic Fuehrer"

definition: The Fascist variety of socialism was called
Zwangswirtschaft -compulsory economy.
All wages, prices, profits, and production quotas
were rigidly controlled by the government.

Americans, Fight Nixonomics with the only effective
philosophic antidote – Laissez Faire Capitalism!

New Right Coalition
330 DARTMOUTH ST. – BOSTON, MASS. 02116

976.

The Almanack of Poor Richard

977.

NIXON

978.

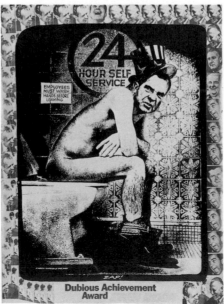

24 HOUR SELF SERVICE

EMPLOYEES
MUST WASH
HANDS BEFORE
LEAVING

Dubious Achievement
Award

979.

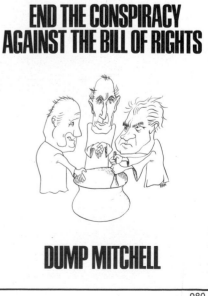

END THE CONSPIRACY
AGAINST THE BILL OF RIGHTS

DUMP MITCHELL

980.

981.

982.

985.

983.

984.

986.

987.

988.

982. U.S.A. 1971.

983. U.S.A. FBI Director J. Edgar Hoover, President Nixon, and Vice President Agnew. Artist: Bob Dara. 1971.

984. U.S.A. Artist: John Miller.

985. U.S.A. "Hookey Spiro." Artist: Bob Dara. 1970.

986. U.S.A. V.P. Agnew. 1970.
Attorney General John Mitchell. 1971.

987. U.S.A. 1970.

988. U.S.A. "Nixon Do." Artist: The Old School. 1971.

989. U.S.A. 1971.

990. U.S.A. 1970.

991. Cuba. Continental Organization of Latin American Students (OCLAE). *Day of support for Vietnam, Cambodia, and Laos: 15-21 October.* 1971.

990.

989.

991.

"Free All Political Prisoners"

994.

LIBERTAD PARA
ANGELA DAVIS
FECH'71

992.

ANGELA DAVIS

993.

I AM A BLACK WOMAN!

שלח את עמי

ОТПУСТИ НАРОД МОЙ

LET MY PEOPLE GO!

995.

LIBERTAD PARA ANGELA DAVIS

996.

992. Chile. *Free Angela Davis '71*. 1971.

993. Cuba. OSPAAAL. 1971.

994. U.S.A. Designed and produced by Richard McCrary. 1971.

995. U.S.A. Student Struggle for Soviet Jewry. 1971.

996. Cuba. The Committee to Free Angela Davis. *Freedom for Angela Davis*. 1971.

997. U.S.A. Student Struggle for Soviet Jewry. 1971.

998. U.S.A. World Federation of the Bergen Belsen Survivors. Artist: S. Hamir. 1970.

שלח את עמי

LET MY PEOPLE GO! שמות ד 16

ОТПУСТИ НАРОД МОЙ

למען עלית יהודי רוסיה לארץ ישראל

Student Struggle for Soviet Jewry
200 WEST 72nd STREET · SUITES 30-31 · NEW YORK, N.Y. 10023
(212) 799-8900

997.

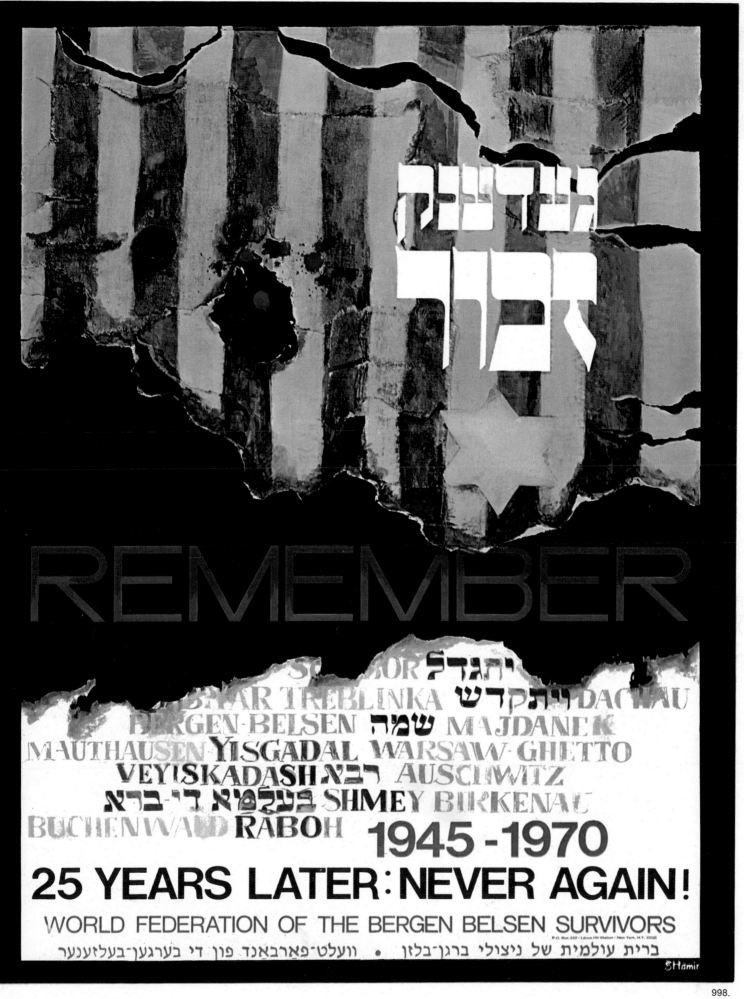

ניט שטעק

יזכור

REMEMBER

SOBIBOR יתגדל
BABI YAR TREBLINKA ויתקדש DACHAU
BERGEN-BELSEN שמה MAJDANEK
MAUTHAUSEN YISGADAL WARSAW-GHETTO
VEYISKADASH רבא AUSCHWITZ
בעלמא די-ברא SHMEY BIRKENAU
BUCHENWALD RABOH 1945-1970
25 YEARS LATER: NEVER AGAIN!
WORLD FEDERATION OF THE BERGEN BELSEN SURVIVORS

P.O. Box 232 · Lenox Hill Station · New York, N.Y. 10028

ברית עולמית של ניצולי ברגן-בלזן • וועלט-פארבאנד פון די בערגען-בעלזענער

SHamir

998.

999. West Germany. *Freedom for Rudolf Hess. Rudolf Hess wanted to end the war. For this must he die in Spandau prison).* 1969.

1000. U.S.A. Robert Shelton, Grand Wizard of the Ku Klux Klan, had been imprisoned for illegal possession of weapons. Graffiti added. 1970.

1001. Chile. *Free Rudolf Hess.* Leaflet poster of unknown origin that was dropped from an airplane during Willy Brandt's visit in Santiago, Chile. 1968.

1002. U.S.A. Black Panther Party. Bobby Seale and Huey Newton, imprisoned Black Panthers.

Solidarity

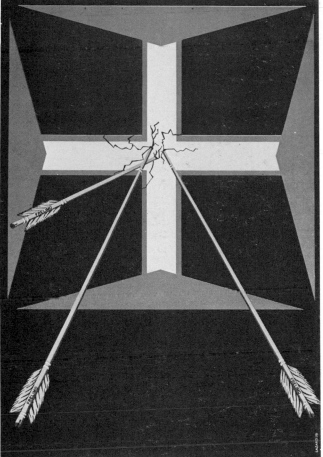

1003. Cuba. Day of solidarity with the people of Mozambique. 1970.

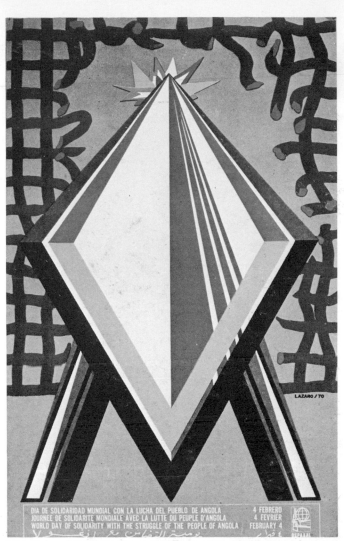

1004. Cuba. OSPAAAL. *Day of solidarity with the struggle of the people of Angola.* 1970.

1005. Italy. International Union of Young Christian Democrats. 1968.

1006. Cuba. OSPAAAL. *Day of solidarity with the people of Laos.*

AUSCHWITZ   BIALYSTOK   RESISTANCE

TUCZYN   LUBLIN   LACHWA

KOVNO   VILNO   TREBLINKA

BIA...   RESISTAN...   SOBIBOR

MINSK   KOV...O

...REBLI...

...CE   AUS...

...TOK   WARSAW

KRAKOW

...ONIN

In memoriam
to the Jewish youth who
fought in the Ghetto uprisings,
WUJS announces

A SEMINAR ON JEWISH RESISTANCE

Lectures, films, discussions on
student response to anti-Semitism,
Jewish youth resistance during
the Second World War,
and Fascism, then and now.

July 12-16, 1971
Reading University
Reading, Berkshire, England

Applications should be sent to:
World Union of Jewish Students
Political Bureau
247 Grays Inn Road
London W.C. 1, England

1007. Great Britain. World Union of Jewish Students. *A Seminar on Jewish Resistance.* 1971.

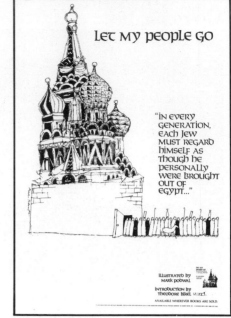

LET MY PEOPLE GO

"IN EVERY
GENERATION,
EACH JEW
MUST REGARD
HIMSELF AS
THOUGH HE
PERSONALLY
WERE BROUGHT
OUT OF
EGYPT..."

ILLUSTRATED BY
MARK PODWAL

INTRODUCTION BY
THEODORE BIKEL

AVAILABLE WHEREVER BOOKS ARE SOLD.

1008. U.S.A. To advertse a Passover Haggadah titled *Let My People Go.* Artist: Mark Podwal. 1972.

1009. Nationalist China. *Strength: The solidarity of the free world.* 1968.

1010. Cuba. 1970.

Aniversario Conferencia Tricontinental
Tricontinental Conference Anniversary
Anniversaire Conférence Tricontinentale

OSPAAAL

1011. Cuba. *OSPAAAL. Day of solidarity with the struggle of the Japanese people.* 1970.

DIA DE SOLIDARIDAD MUNDIAL CON LA LUCHA DEL PUEBLO JAPONES 6 de agosto
DAY OF WORLD SOLIDARITY WITH THE STRUGGLE OF THE JAPANESE PEOPLE August 6
JOURNEE DE SOLIDARITE MONDIALE AVEC LA LUTTE DU PEUPLE JAPONAIS 6 août

HIROSHIMA

1012. U.S.A. Radio Free Europe. 1971.

1013. U.S.A. UNICEF. *A future for every child.* 1971.

1014. Great Britain. International Union of Students. 1970.

1015. U.S.A. 1969.

1016. *Revolution till victory.*

1017. U.S.A. The Coca-Cola Company. 1968.

SECTION V.
Poster Substitutes

The few selections shown here only hint at the proliferation and pervasiveness of propaganda graphics today. Although these substitutes may replace the poster in some cases, they for the most part reinforce the poster's function and provide additional insurance through visual saturation.

BUTTONS

1018. 1019. 1020. 1021. 1022. 1023.
1024. 1025. 1026. 1027. 1028. 1029.
1030. 1031. 1032. 1033. 1034. 1035.
1036. 1037. 1038. 1039. 1040. 1041.

1018. U.S.A. New Mobilization Committee. 1969.
1019. U.S.A. Young Socialist Alliance. Hammer and sickle. 1969.
1020. China. Mao button.
1021. U.S.A. Black power. 1971.
1022. U.S.A. Free Angela (Davis). 1970.
1023. U.S.A. Candidate George Bush. 1970.
1024. U.S.A. 1971.
1025. U.S.A. Student Mobilization Committee. U.S. troops out of Southeast Asia. 1970.
1026. U.S.A. Student Mobilization Committee. 1970.
1027. U.S.A. Urban League. Give a damn (about civil rights). 1970.
1028. U.S.A. Young Americans for Freedom. 1969.
1029. U.S.A. Young Americans for Freedom. 1959.

1030. U.S.A. Young Americans for Freedom. 1969.
1031. U.S.A. Young Americans for Freedom. 1969.
1032. U.S.A. 1970.
1033. U.S.A. 1970.
1034. U.S.A. 1970.
1035. U.S.A. 1970.
1036. U.S.A. 1970.
1037. Denmark. Conservative Party. *For the Future*. 1970.
1038. France. Young Socialists. 1969.
1039. U.S.A. Young Americans for Freedom. 1969.
1040. U.S.A. United Klans of America. Never (integration). 1969.
1041. U.S.A. 1970.

PATCHES

1042. U.S.A. United Klans of America. Sign of the Klans. 1970.

1043. Australia, Labor Party. 1968.

1044. U.S.A. United Klans of America (UKA). 1969.

1045. U.S.A. Ecology symbol. Designer: Ron Chereskin. 1971.

BUMPERSTICKERS

I AM A SECRET MEMBER OF THE JOHN BIRCH SOCIETY
1046.

FRAMÅT MED KDS
1047.

REMEMBER THE PUEBLO
1048.

VICTORY IN VIETNAM
THE UNTRIED ALTERNATIVE
1049.

JOIN MOVEMENT TO RESTORE DECENCY "MOTOREDE"
Write P.O. Box 8352
San Marino, California 91108
1050.

UKA
1051.

you win with NDP
1052.

NEVER UKA
1053.

REGISTER COMMUNISTS NOT GUNS!
1054.

MY GOD IS NOT DEAD .... SORRY 'BOUT YOURS !
1055.

SUPPORT YOUR LOCAL POLICE KEEP THEM INDEPENDENT!
1056.

Vote Column "F" Nov. 4th FIGHT FOR "FREEDOM!" NATIONAL CONSERVATIVE PARTY
Paid for by Hudson County Conservative Club, Weehawken
1057.

THE SYMBOL OF... WHITE POWER NIGGERS BEWARE! HANDS OFF WHITES!...or DIE! AMERICAN NAZI PARTY (NATIONAL SOCIALIST WHITE PEOPLE'S PARTY)
Nat'l HQ, Box 5505, Arlington, Va. — Dallas HQ, Box 3960, Dallas, Texas.
1058.

...TOGETHERNESS... LABOR & HHH
1059.

BOYCOTT COMPULSION: NOT GRAPES
1060.

ANOTHER DEMOCRAT FOR NIXON
Official Nixon Material — Sales & Wheeler, Inc.
1061.

1046. U.S.A. John Birch Society. 1970.
1047. Sweden. Christian Democratic Party (KDS). *Forward with* (KDS).
1048. U.S.A. Young Americans for Freedom. Capture of the S.S." Pueblo" by North Korea. 1969.
1049. U.S.A. National Student Committee for Victory in Vietnam. 1969.
1050. U.S.A. Movement to Restore Decency. 1969.
1051. U.S.A. United Klans of America (UKA). 1970.
1052. Canada. New Democratic Party (NDP). 1968.
1053. U.S.A. United Klans of America. Never (integration). 1970.

1054. U.S.A. John Birch Society. 1970.
1055. U.S.A. 1969.
1056. U.S.A. 1969.
1057. U.S.A. National Conservative Party. 1968.
1058. U.S.A. American Nazi Party.
1059. U.S.A. Democratic Party. Hubert H. Humphrey running for President. 1968.
1060. U.S.A. 1969.
1061. U.S.A. 1968.

1062. Ireland.
Fine Gail.
1970.

1063. France.
Democratic Union
of the Republic.
(UDR). Blotter.

1064. U.S.A. 1971.

1065. Ireland. Labour Party. 1970.

1066. Netherlands. Committee for Assistance to Vietnam.
1968.

1067. U.S.A. 1971.

1068. U.S.A. Young Lords Party. Long Live Puerto Rico.
1971.

1069. U.S.A. Socialist Workers Party. 1968.

1070. U.S.A. United Klans of America (UKA).
Business card. 1970.

1071. U.S.A. United Klans of America (UKA).
Business card. 1970.

1072. U.S.A. National Peace
Action Coalition. 1970.

1073. U.S.A. National Socialist White People's Party.
1970.

1074. Origin unknown.

1075. U.S.A. 1970.

1077. U.S.A. Ballpoint pen. 1970.

1076. Italy. Republican Party (PRI). Paper banner. 1970.

1078. U.S.S.R. Writing pad with picture of Lenin. 1967.

1079. U.S.A. Liberal Party. New York City. John V. Lindsay running for mayor. Matchbox. 1969.

1080. U.S.A. *Stormtrooper Magazine*. Newspaper advertisement. 1970.

1081. South Vietnam. Safe-conduct pass. 1971.

1082. U.S.A. Ronald Reagan. Dart board. 1970.

1083. License Plate. U.S.A. 1969.

1084. U.S.A. Peace and Freedom Party. Dick Gregory running for President. Fake dollar bill. 1968.

MISCELLANEOUS

1085. U.S.A. "Potty poster." 1971.

1086. U.S.A.
Republican Party.
Richard M. Nixon
running for President.

FOR THE FREEDOM
OF NATIONS!

FOR THE FREEDOM
OF THE
INDIVIDUALS!

DM
EINE

ABN

ANTIBÓLSHEVIK BLOC
OF NATIONS

1087. Anti-Bolshevik League. Leaflet.

Adolf Hitler

A Bust of the Leader

Faithfully Reproduced in Baked Ceramicware
Excellent Quality & Detail
Felt Padded Base

Choose from two colors

● Deep Bronze (Matt Finish)
● Bright Gold

$5.50 each

Order from
NS PUBLICATIONS
Box 5505 — Arlington, Virginia 22205

Add 10% on all orders to cover costs of packaging and mailing

1088. U.S.A. National Socialist White
People's Party. Advertisement for bust
of Hitler. 1970.

1089. France.
Center
Democratic Party.
Jean Lecanuet.
Key chain.
1969.

С праздником,
товарищи!

1090. U.S.S.R. *New Year's Greetings, Comrades.* 1967.

1091. U.S.A. Republican Party. Spiro Agnew running for Vice President. Watch. 1970.

1092. U.S.A. American Independent Party. George C. Wallace running for President. Plastic hat. 1968.

1093. U.S.A. Democratic nomination for President. Lunch boxes. 1968.

1094. Cuba. New Year Greeting Card, published by Radio Havana. 1970.

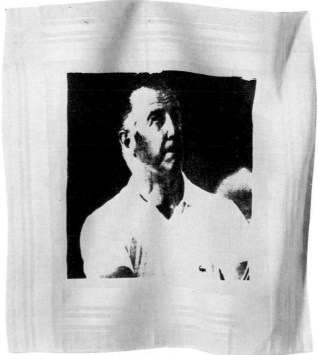

1095. U.S.A. Democratic Party. Hubert H. Humphrey campaigning for Democratic nomination for President. Shopping bag. 1968.

1096. U.S.A. Republican Party. Spiro Agnew running for Vice President. Handkerchief. 1970.

NOTES

Page 21
Lloyd Garrison, "Political Sides Form a World Unit," *New York Times,* 23 November 1968, 40.

Page 21
The opinion was given to the author by John d'Arc Lorenz, a campaign consultant for the firm of Cyr, Picard & Associates, Washington, D.C., in an interview 7 June 1969.

Page 22
Ervine Metzl, *The Poster: Its History and Its Art* (New York: Watson-Guptill, 1963), 177.

Page 22
Franz Goess and Manfred Beer, *Prager Anschläge* (Frankfurt: Ullstein, 1968), 14.

Page 23
Harold F. Hutchinson, *The Poster as Illustrated History from 1860.* New York: Viking, 1968, 12.

Page 23
The Christian Democrats of Italy, for example, reported using 12,500,-000 posters in the 1968 parliamentary elections alone.

Page 26
G. Demosfenova, *Sovetski Politicheski Plakat* / The Soviet Political Poster / Moscow: Obche redakzi F. Kaloshina, "Iskustva Moskva Isdatelstva," 1968, 14.

Page 26
Horst Reiman, *Wahlplakate.* Heidelberg: Brausbruck, 1961.

Page 27
Viktor Semenovich, *Kak Sozdaetsia Plakat* / How to Design a Poster / Moscow: Isdatelstva Akademii Hudoshjest U.S.S.R., 1963.

Page 27
Arno Scholz, *Das Einmaleins der politische Werbung.* Berlin-Grünewald: Arani, 1959.

Page 27
Scholz, *Das Einmaleins,* 38.

Page 27
Erwin Schockel, *Das politische Plakat: Eine psychologische Betrachtung.* Munich: Der Schriftenreihe der Reichspropagandaleitung der Zentraverlag der NSDAP, Franz Eher Nachs, 1939.

Page 28
Haig A. Bosmajian, "The Role of the Political Poster in Hitler's Rise to Power." *Print,* May 1966, 28-31.

Page 28
Schockel, *Das politische Plakat,* 10.

Page 28
Edward Conrad Janicik, *Art as Propaganda, With Emphasis on Iconographic Aspects.* Ann Arbor, Mich.: University Microfilms, 1956.

Page 30
Louis F. Peters, *Kunst und Revolte, Das politsche Plakat und der franzoesischen Studenten* / Art and Revolt: The Political Poster and the French Rebellion / Cologne: DuMont Schauberg, 1968.

Page 30
Dugald Stermer, *The Art of Revolution: Castro's Cuba, 1959-1970.* Introduction by Susan Sontag. New York: McGraw-Hill, 1970.

Page 30
Susan Sontag, introduction to *Art of Revolution,* ii.

Page 30
Dugald Stermer, "The Agit Pop Art of Cuba," *Ramparts,* 14-28 December 1968.

Page 31
Genevieve Morel, "Poster Politics in Red China," *Réalitiés.* November 1968.

Page 31
Gary D. Yanker, "Prop-Art," *Print,* February 1970.

Page 31
Adolf Hitler, *Mein Kampf,* trans. Ralph Mannheim. Boston: Little, Brown, 1943, 180.

Page 31
Reiman, *Wahlplakate* 7.

Page 33
Young & Rubicam, *How to Make Posters.*

Page 33
Young & Rubicam, *How to Make Posters That Will Win the War.* New York, 1942.

Page 33
Statements attributed to Lorenz represent the research, application, and conclusions of Cyr, Picard, & Associates, campaign consultants and political researchers, 3600 M Street, N.W., Washington, D.C., as related to the atuhor in an interview with Lorenz 7 June 1969 and a subsequent letter 11 June 1969.

Page 33
Schockel, *Das politische Plakat,* 14.

Page 33
Schockel, *Das politische Plakat,* 172.

Page 35
Louis F. Peters, *Kunst und Revolte, Das politische Plakat und der Aufstand der franzoesischen Studenten.* Cologne: DuMont Schauberg, 1968, 9.

Page 35
Josiah Reinhardt, "Posters: Begin Your Exciting Art Collection Now," *Art International, December 1967,* 248-49.

Page 35
Schockel, *Das politische Plakat,* 150.

Page 40
Cyr, Picard.

Page 40
Schockel, *Das politische Plakat,* 7.

Page 40
Peters, *Kunst und Revolte,* 10.

Page 40
Peters, *Kunst und Revolte,* 7.

Page 40
Schockel, *Das politische Plakat,* 8.

Page 40
Schockel, *Das politische Plakat,* 9.

Page 45
Schockel, *Das politische Plakat,* 58.

Page 46
Schockel, *Das politische Plakat,* 30.

Page 46
Schockel, *Das politische Plakat,* 34.

Page 46
Scholz, *Das Einmaleins,* 39.

Page 46
Schockel, *Das politische Plakat,* 17.

Page 47
Morel, "Poster Politics in Red China," 38.

Page 58
Gerald Holtam, *Win,* October 1969.

Page 60
Janicik, *Art as Propaganda,* 191.

Page 62
Schockel, *Das politische Plakat,* 221.

Page 63
Schockel, *Das politische Plakat,* 138.

Page 68
Harold Lasswell, *Psychopathology and Politics*, New York: Viking 1960; *Politics: Who Gets What, When and How*. New York: Meridian, 1958; *World Revolutionary Elites*. Cambridge, Mass.: MIT Press, 1966.

Page 72
Peters, *Kunst und Revolte*, 68-73.

Page 76
Stermer, *The Art of Revolution*, 34.

Page 79
See *1970 Campaign Handbook,* published by the Democratic National Committee.

Page 80
People v. *Yolen,* 267 NYS 2d 25, 1966.

Page 80
Blackwell v. *Issaquena County Board of Education,* 363 F. 2d 744, 1966.

Page 80
Burnside v. *Byars,* 363 F. 2d 744, 1966.

Page 80
Blackwell, 751.

Page 80
Kissinger v. *New York City Transit Authority,* F. Supp. 438, S.D.N.Y., 1967.

Page 81
Hillside Community Church v. *City of Tacoma,* 455 P. 2d 350, 1969.

Page 81
Wirta v. *Alameda-Contra Costa Transit,* 434 P. 2d 982, 1967

BIBLIOGRAPHY

Articles

Bosmajian, Haig A. "The Role of the Political Poster in Hitler's Rise to Power." *Print,* May 1966, 28-31.
Garrison, Lloyd. "Political Aides Form a World Unit." *New York Times,* 23 November, 1968, 40.
Morel, Genevieve. "Poster Politics In Red China." *Réalitiés,* 1968, 35-39.
Reinhardt, Josiah. "Posters, Begin Your Exciting Art Collection Now."
Art International, December 1967, 248-49.
Secrest, Meryle. "Poster Popularity: Writing Is On The Wall." *The Washington Post,* 4 May, 1969, K1 and K8.
Stermer, Dugald. "The Agit Pop Art of Cuba." *Ramparts,* 14-28. December, 1968, 32-37.
Yanker, Gary D. "Prop-Art." *Print,* February 1970, 35-41.

Books

Arnold, Friedrich. *Anschläge: Deutche Plakate als Dokumente der Zeit* 1900-1960. Ebenhausen bei München: Sangewische Brandt, 1953.
Atelier Populaire. *Posters From The Revolution:* Paris, May 1968. Indianapolis: Bobbs-Merrill, 1969.
Berger, John. *Art and Revolution: Ernest Neizvestny and the Role of the Artist in the U.S.S.R.* New York: Pantheon, 1969.
Demosfenova, G. *Sovetski Politicheski Plakat.* [The Soviet Political Poster]. Moscow: Obche redakzi F. Kaloshina, "Iskustva Moskva Isdatelstva," 1968.
DeWitt, J. Doyle. *A Century of Campaign Buttons 1789-1889.* Hartford, Conn.: Travelers Press, 1959.
Experimentalle Analyse der Plakatwirkung. Vienna: Osterreichische Werbewissenschaftliche Gesellschaft, 1959.
Gehrig, Oscar. *Plakatkunst und Revolution.* Berlin: Wasmuth, 1919.
Hardie, Martin, and Sabin, A. K. *War Posters Issued by Belligerent and Neutral Nations, 1914-1919.* London. A. & C. Black, 1930.
Hitler, Adolf. *Mein Kampf.* Translated by Ralph Mannheim. Boston: Houghton Mifflin, 1943.
Hutchinson, Harold F. *The Poster as Illustrated History from 1860.* New York: Viking, 1968.
Ivanov, Viktor Semenovich, *Kak Sozdaetsia Plakat.* [How to Design a Poster]. Moscow: Isdatelstva Akademii Hudoshjest U.S.S.R., 1963.
Janicik, Edward Conrad. *Art as Propaganda, With Emphasis on Iconographic Aspects,* Ph.D. thesis, University of Pittsburgh, 1956. Ann Arbor: University Microfilms.
Luscomb, Sally C. *The Collectors Encyclopedia of Buttons,* New York: Crown, 1967.
Massiczek, Albert and Sagl, Herman. *Zeit An Der Wand.* Vienna: Europa, 1967.
McLuhan, Marshall. *Understanding Media.* New York: McGraw-Hill, 1964.
Metzl, Ervine. *The Poster: Its History and Its Art.* New York: Watson-Guptill, 1963.
Peters, Louis F. *Kunst und Revolte: Das Politische Plakat und der Aufstand der franzoesischen Studenten.* Cologne: DuMont Schauberg, 1968.
Pennell, Joseph. *Joseph Pennell's Liberty-Loan Poster.* Philadelphia: Lippincott, 1918.
Politische Plakate der Gegenwart. Edited by R. Gruhlich and J. Hampel. Munich: Bruchmann and Günter Olzog, 1971.
Price, Charles M. *How to Put in Patriotic Posters the Stuff that Makes People Stop—Look—Act.* Washington, D.C.: National Committee of Patriotic Societies, 1918.
Reiman, Horst *Wahlplakate.* Heidelberg: Brausbruck, 1961.
Rickards, Maurice. *Posters of Protest And Revolution.* New York: Walker, 1970.
Schockel, Erwin. *Das politische Plakat: Eine psychologische Betrachtung.* Munich: Der Schriftenreihe der Reichsprogandaleitung der Zentralverlag der NSDAP, Franz Eber Nachs, 1939.
Scholz, Arno. *Das Einmaleins der politische Werbung.* Berlin-Grünewald: Arani, 1959.
Stermer, Dugald. *The Art of Revolution: Castro's Cuba, 1959-1970.* Introduction by Susan Sontag. New York: McGraw-Hill, 1970.
Tertz, Abraham. *On Socialist Realism.* New York: Pantheon, 1960.
Young & Rubicam, Inc. *How to Make Posters That Will Win The War.* New York, 1942.

CREDITS

INDEX